Solutions for
LDS Families

Solutions for LDS Families

24 Weekly Lessons to Strengthen Your Family at Home

Paula Noble Fellingham

Covenant Communications, Inc.

Published by Covenant Communications, Inc.
American Fork, Utah

Printed in the United States of America
First Printing: August 2003

08 07 06 05 04 03 02 01   10 9 8 7 6 5 4 3 2 1

ISBN 1-59156-289-9

I give heartfelt thanks to those who are the wind beneath my wings: my wonderful husband Gil; our precious children and their eternal companions—Missy and Darin, Angela and Darrel, Joy and Steve, Elise and Les, Danny, David, and Benjamin; my dear parents Wendell and Gwen Noble; and the ultimate solution for families—our loving Heavenly Father and Jesus Christ.

TABLE OF CONTENTS

TO THE READER

Throughout the world the stability of the family is weakening. Increased marital infidelity, crime, teen pregnancy, and addictions to alcohol, drugs, and pornography pervade our society in epidemic proportions. President Spencer W. Kimball stated, "Many of the social restraints which in the past have helped to reinforce and to shore up the family are dissolving and disappearing. The time will come when only those who believe deeply and actively in the family will be able to preserve their families in the midst of the gathering evil around us" (*Ensign,* Nov. 1980, 4).

Yet signs of hope abound. Many recognize today's moral decay as fulfillment of scripture and they stand boldly on the Lord's side. Our dedicated missionary force increases in number and strength, as does our membership. More and more people around the world are hearkening to the Shepherd's voice as He beckons, "Come, follow me" (Luke 18:22).

Elder Joseph B. Wirthlin of the Quorum of the Twelve Apostles remarked, "If you build your homes on the foundation rock of our Redeemer and the gospel, they can be sanctuaries where your families can be sheltered from the raging storms of life" (*Ensign,* May 1993, 71).

Solutions for LDS Families offers ways to build upon that firm foundation and strengthen family relationships. It begins with a survey designed to help family members understand one another's honest feelings. Twenty-four lessons are then presented in a manner that every family can use. In each lesson the concept, discussion, activity, and assignment are explained in easy-to-understand terms. All lessons relate to the statements in the survey and include additional activities for family enjoyment.

When the material in *Solutions for LDS Families* is used in homes where there is a desire for improvement, wonderful changes will occur. Families will experience increased love and peace, and relationships will be strengthened in powerful ways. Strong families can build strong individuals, and those individuals can build the kind of world we all dream of.

The good news is that there are solutions.

It's time for solutions.

Introduction

How glorious and challenging is our parental stewardship to love, teach, and protect Heavenly Father's children during this, the final dispensation of the fullness of times!

Elder M. Russell Ballard of the Quorum of the Twelve Apostles taught, "Every human being is a spirit child of God and lived with Heavenly Father before coming to Earth. He entrusts His spirit children to earthly parents, who provide a mortal body for them through the miracle of physical birth, and gives to parents the sacred opportunity and responsibility to love, protect, teach, and to bring them up in light and truth so they may one day, through the Atonement and Resurrection of Jesus Christ, return to our Father's presence" (*Ensign,* May 1991, 78).

Returning to our heavenly home with our entire family is a primary goal for Latter-day Saints. Yet the path home is often difficult and perilous. Although we're blessed with modern-day revelation, abundant resources, and righteous leadership, we still struggle. Daily we seek answers to personal and family challenges.

Let me assure you that I know, without doubt, that the answer to our every question lies within the restored gospel of Jesus Christ. Our Lord and Savior is the way. In Him is all light and truth, and I am grateful beyond words for our Savior's love and atoning sacrifice. It is by Him and through Him that we can gain eternal life. This book is designed as a tool to strengthen families and to help them return, all together, to the presence of our heavenly parents.

A source of great joy in my life is seeking and discovering solutions for my family—solutions that I can then share with others. Many times while writing this book, I wanted to sit right down next to you and talk face-to-face. I am sincerely interested in you and your family. I delight in your successes, and I would like to help lighten whatever load you carry. With all of my heart I care about strengthening families—yours and mine.

As we begin the adventure of finding solutions, I would like you to feel secure in the knowledge of four things:

> *First,* no matter how unfortunate your past has been—regardless of how many people have failed you in life—you can begin today to make choices that will result in secure, loving relationships.

> *Second,* finding solutions to problems usually requires a willingness to change, learn, and unselfishly do "whatever it takes." Change must come from the inside out. No set of rules or suggestions from a book will make a difference unless minds are open and hearts are soft.

Third, because families are groups of individuals, when each family member improves, the whole family becomes stronger. Finding solutions sometimes requires individuals to sacrifice for the good of the family. Happily, the result of working together to reach common goals is increased harmony, unity, and love.

Fourth, creating a successful family is a day-by-day (sometimes minute-by-minute) effort. Finding solutions to individual and family problems is a process that takes time and considerable effort. My heartfelt suggestion is to be kind to yourself and patient with your family on your solution-seeking journey. Don't expect immediate success. Remember that there is no perfect family, and there are no perfect parents. The key is to learn from mistakes and to keep trying. The rewards of your efforts will be priceless.

HOW TO USE THIS BOOK

It is my hope and desire that this book will be a blessing to your family as you become familiar and comfortable with it and use it regularly in your home.

There are four parts to *Solutions for LDS Families:* Getting Started, Introduction for Parents, Lessons, and Solutions through Stories and Poems.

It is vitally important that you begin by reading the Getting Started section. To omit this part of the book would be like trying to build a home without a foundation. There are four important steps to Getting Started: the Family Survey, the Family Contract, the Family Home Evening, and the Family Mission Statement. Take your time with these exercises. They can be powerful tools to help you build relationships and strengthen your family.

The Introduction for Parents section is found at the beginning of each chapter. It introduces the subject of the chapter and the four lessons that follow. It is an opportunity for me to speak to parents about the subject of that chapter prior to the lessons they will teach the family. Parents can share information from the Introduction for Parents to enhance the lessons if they so desire.

The twenty-four lessons in this book reflect the twenty-four questions in the Family Survey. The lessons all follow the same format: follow-up from the previous lesson; a concept; family survey review; story and discussion; and activity and assignment. Several lessons have additional activities and/or additional solutions for success. The lessons are to be given by a family member (written in a style that can be read out loud to even younger children), and, as much as possible, every person in the family should participate. For example, one person could read the concept, another family member could share the story and lead the discussion on it, and another could help with the activity and assignment exercises. Of course, families can use the lessons however they'd like—there is certainly no wrong way to do it. The key is to meet regularly and use the lessons in whatever way is best for your family.

Solutions through Stories and Poems is a section found at the end of each chapter. These highlight the lessons and are wonderful teaching tools. I thought your family might enjoy some additional stories and poems for those evenings when you have just a little extra time to spend together. Or perhaps you might enjoy reading them instead of a lesson once in a while. Whatever you choose, the stories and poems are intended to be additional resources, designed to strengthen individuals and families.

Finally, I wanted to share some thoughts about the research upon which this book is based. *Solutions for LDS Families* is based on the research of three family specialists: Dr.

Thomas R. Lee, Utah State University professor and Extension Family Relations Specialist; and Drs. Ivan F. Beutler and Wesley R. Burr, professors of Family Science at Brigham Young University. The study they completed, which had profound relevance for this book, is titled "Kindness and Unkindness in Families," and a version of it appears in *Psychological Reports Journal*.[1] These researchers concluded that kindness is the single most important ingredient in a happy home. They define kindness as "being gentle, caring, charitable, and concerned for the long-term welfare of others."[2] The study goes on to say that "kindness and unkindness are not roles or tasks people have, but rather they are *ways of being,* ways people relate as they go about their various activities, tasks, and roles."[3] This tells me that if we are "gentle, caring, charitable, and concerned for the long-term welfare of others" in our thoughts, words, and actions, we will contribute to the happiness and effectiveness of our family and will be good examples of kindness.

Could it be that something as simple as kindness is the key to individual and family happiness? As we "go about our various activities, tasks, and roles" in life, is kindness a virtue that pervades our thoughts, permeates our words, and shows in our actions? I understand that being kind can often be very difficult. However, the idea that kindness is a foundation piece in a happy home causes me to believe that finding solutions for families is a reachable goal. When I first heard this concept, I thought, "I can do this! I can learn to show kindness to my family and others." And I am hoping you will feel the same way.

The scriptures are filled with passages on the importance of showing loving-kindness. Countless stories and sermons profess this virtue's eternal significance. Therefore, I chose loving-kindness as the foundational value of this book. Indeed, it overarches and underscores every lesson.

Jesus Christ, our Lord and Redeemer, *is* loving-kindness. In the Introduction for Parents in Chapter One I highlight just a few examples of the kindness Christ showed during His mortal ministry. How marvelous is God's assurance that "with everlasting kindness will I have mercy on thee . . . For the mountains shall depart, and the hills be removed; but my kindness shall not depart from thee . . . saith the Lord" (Isa. 54:8, 10).

As I read this scripture, my heart swells with gratitude for the Lord's everlasting kindness to His children. I am reminded once again of our parental stewardship and responsibilities: to follow His example and shower our children with loving-kindness; to "teach them to love one another, and to serve one another" (Mosiah 4:15); and, as the offspring of a loving Heavenly Father, to heed His counsel and "be ye kind one to another" (Eph. 4:32).

Now, let us begin the journey of finding solutions for the challenges families face. And please remember, during every step of the way, that we need to be kind and patient with ourselves and family members as we embark on the wonderful adventure of strengthening our families.

Paula Noble Fellingham

GETTING STARTED

Four important steps of *Solutions for LDS Families* will get you started. As you read and participate in these steps, your family will have a good start in laying the foundation of mutual understanding, organization, and unity.

1. FAMILY SURVEY

- In the survey each family member responds to statements about your family life.

- After you take the survey and discuss the responses, you'll see how family members really view your family.

- The survey will help you better understand one another. It will show your family strengths, and it will also reveal some things you may want to improve.

2. FAMILY CONTRACT

- This is a contract that family members sign indicating their willingness to participate in the *Solutions for LDS Families* activities.

- Long-term success begins with a firm commitment.

3. FAMILY HOME EVENING

- Holding regular family meetings is the best way to be organized as a family.

- Family home evenings have three parts: family council, lesson, and activity.

- This is a good time for families to gather and share their feelings, plan, learn, and play.

4. FAMILY MISSION STATEMENT

- A family mission statement is like your family constitution. It's a statement of your family's beliefs and goals.

- A mission statement defines your family rules and values.

- With a family mission statement you'll have direction, and you'll feel more like a team working together.

You can begin the *Solutions for LDS Families* activities by reading the Family Survey Instructions on the following page, then taking the Family Survey.

FAMILY SURVEY INSTRUCTIONS

The Family Survey is designed to help families understand one another's feelings and how each person views the family. When all family members honestly respond to the survey statements and talk about the results with kindness, the survey can be a powerful tool for family growth.

Each one of the twenty-four lessons in *Solutions for LDS Families* relates directly to the statements in the Family Survey. For example, Lesson One, Kind Thoughts, corresponds to statement one in the survey: "Our family thinks kind thoughts about one another." Completing the survey as a family will give you a basic understanding of how family members feel about the issues you will later address in the lessons. This will aid in your lesson preparation and serve as a guide for your discussions.

There are two very important things to remember when you complete the survey and discuss the results: First, family members need to respond to the statements with complete honesty. Tell how you really feel. Second, when your family talks about the answers given in the survey, make only positive comments. No family members should be made to feel guilty or challenged because of their honest responses.

Each family member needs his or her own copy of the survey. You may also photocopy the survey found on page 7. To complete the survey, follow these four steps:

1. **Respond to each survey statement twice.** The way you respond is by putting either 1 almost never), 3 (sometimes), or 5 (almost always) beside each statement.

   • First, respond by thinking about the way your family is right now (actual).

   • Second, respond by thinking about the way you would like it to be (ideal).

   • Third, total these numbers. You'll see that the statements address six areas of family life: kindness, commitment, communication, choices, well-being, and spirituality.

2. **Calculate the results of all family members' responses.** On the left, write each family member's name. Write each person's totals in the chart for each of the six areas. Add all numbers (actual and ideal). Write the average number below the totals. You'll get the average number by dividing your total by the number of people in your family. For example, if the total number is 50, divide by 5 people in your family, and the average number is 10.

3. **Graph the results.** Using your average actual numbers, put a dot on the graph above each of the six areas—put the dot on the graph's vertical dotted line. Connect the dots. Now put x's across the graph, using your average ideal numbers. Connect the x's. You have two graphs: the actual way your family is now and the ideal way you'd like to be.

FAMILY SURVEY

Name_____

Choose the number below that you think is the most correct for each statement. On the left, respond to the statement by marking the way you think your family is now (actual). On the right, respond the way you would like your family to be (ideal).

Almost Never	**Sometimes**	**Almost Always**
1	3	5

Actual   Ideal

_____ 1.   Our family thinks kind thoughts about one another.   _____
_____ 2.   In our family we express love for each other.   _____
_____ 3.   We use a kind tone of voice when we speak.   _____
_____ 4.   We treat one another the way we like to be treated.   _____
_____ 5.   We enjoy doing things together as a family.   _____
_____ 6.   We set family goals together.   _____
_____ 7.   Our family helps one another without being asked.   _____
_____ 8.   We have family traditions.   _____
_____ 9.   We try to understand one another's feelings.   _____
_____ 10. We speak kindly to one another and try not to criticize.   _____
_____ 11. We listen to each other.   _____
_____ 12. In our family we can say what we feel.   _____
_____ 13. We take responsibility for our own mistakes.   _____
_____ 14. We all help make the rules in our family.   _____
_____ 15. We try to prevent problems before they occur.   _____
_____ 16. We can talk about things without arguing.   _____
_____ 17. Our family has good health habits.   _____
_____ 18. We enjoy learning in our family.   _____
_____ 19. Our family enjoys being with other people.   _____
_____ 20. Our family makes wise financial decisions.   _____
_____ 21. We believe and live the principles of the gospel.   _____
_____ 22. Our family prays together.   _____
_____ 23. We worship Heavenly Father as a family.   _____
_____ 24. We share the gospel with others.   _____

_____ **Total**   **Total**_____

FAMILY SURVEY RESULTS

Name: _____

Step 2

Beside each statement number, write your actual and ideal responses.

Results of Individual Responses

Solutions

	Kindness		Commitment		Communication		Choices		Well-Being		Spirituality	
	Actual	Ideal	Actual	Ideal	Actual	Ideal	Actual	Ideal	Actual	Ideal	Actual	Ideal
Statement # 1			5		9		13		17		21		
Statement # 2			6		10		14		18		22		
Statement # 3			7		11		15		19		23		
Statement # 4			8		12		16		20		24		
Totals												

Step 3

Write the totals for each person beside his name. Write the totals and averages at the bottom.

Results of all Family Members' Responses

Family Members' Names	Actual	Ideal	Actual	Ideal	Actual	Ideal	Actual	Ideal	Actual	Ideal	Actual	Ideal
Totals												
Averages												

Step 4

Using your average actual numbers, put a dot on the graph above each area on the Vertical lines.

Using your average ideal numbers put X's on the vertical lines.

Connect all the dots and X's with a line.

Graph of Results

Kindness	Commitment	Communication	Choices	Well-Being	Spirituality
20	20	20	20	20	20
15	15	15	15	15	15
10	10	10	10	10	10
5	5	5	5	5	5

| Kindness | Commitment | Communication | Choices | Well-Being | Spirituality |

FAMILY SURVEY RESULTS

Example

Name: Linda

Step 2	Results of Individual Responses																
Beside each statement number, write your actual and ideal responses.	**Solutions**																
		Kindness			Commitment			Communication			Choices			Well-Being			Spirituality	
		Actual	Ideal		Actual	Ideal		Actual	Ideal		Actual	Ideal		Actual	Ideal		Actual	Ideal
Statement # 1		3	5	5	3	5	9	3	5	13	1	5	17	3	5	21	3	5
Statement # 2		3	5	6	1	5	10	3	5	14	3	5	18	3	5	22	3	5
Statement # 3		3	5	7	1	5	11	1	3	15	3	5	19	3	5	23	3	5
Statement # 4		3	5	8	3	3	12	3	5	16	3	5	20	3	5	24	1	5
Totals		12	20		8	18		10	18		10	20		12	20		10	20

Step 3
Write the totals for each person beside his name. Write the totals and averages at the bottom.

	Results of all Family Members' Responses											
Family Members' Names	Actual	Ideal	Actual	Ideal	Actual	Ideal	Actual	Ideal	Actual	Ideal	Actual	Ideal
Mom	16	20	18	20	16	20	12	20	14	20	14	20
Dad	18	20	16	20	14	20	10	20	12	20	14	20
Linda	12	20	8	18	10	18	10	20	12	20	10	18
Tom	10	20	10	18	12	20	8	20	10	20	10	20
Totals	56	80	52	76	52	78	40	80	48	80	48	78
Averages	14	20	13	19	13	19	10	20	12	20	12	19

Step 4

Using your average actual numbers, put a dot on the graph above each area on the Vertical lines.

Using your average ideal numbers put X's on the vertical lines.

Connect all the dots and X's with a line.

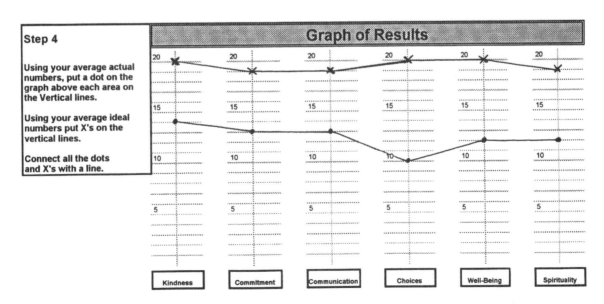

| Kindness | Commitment | Communication | Choices | Well-Being | Spirituality |

AFTER THE FAMILY SURVEY

Completing the Family Survey is an important first step in the *Solutions for LDS Families* plan. This survey can become a valuable tool for your family as you discuss your responses throughout the lessons.

Family members need to understand that it is perfectly all right to have different responses. There are no "right" or "wrong" responses. Family members' numbers will often be different because individuals have different beliefs and perceptions. These differences can be very useful in discussing problems and possible solutions.

Take some time now to discuss your responses. Talk about how the statements made you feel. Remember to make only positive comments toward others' answers during your family discussion.

If you've chosen to complete the graphs, you should have two graphs. One line shows where you are now as a family (actual). The other line shows where you'd like to be (ideal).

As a family, look at your graphs. Consider your results and talk about each of these questions:

- How do we feel about the kindness we show to one another?

- How well do we commit our time to each other and to the family?

- How well do we communicate in our family?

- How do we feel about the choices we make?

- How is our family's physical, mental, social, and financial well-being?

- How is our spirituality?

Look at your graphs again. Talk about where you are today and where you want to be. Decide which areas you want to work on first, then set three family goals. List them on the following page.

FAMILY SURVEY GOALS

Based on your results from the Family Survey, list the goals your family wants to reach.

GOAL #1 _____

_____

_____

GOAL #2 _____

_____

_____

GOAL #3 _____

_____

_____

FAMILY CONTRACT

The Family Contract is on the following page. When you sign this contract you are committing your heart and your time to finding solutions that can powerfully strengthen your family. You are pledging your willingness to participate in the *Solutions for LDS Families* lessons and activities.

A concept, discussion, activity, and assignment are explained in each of the twenty-four lessons. It is best to approach the lessons with open minds; be willing to learn and grow together. With this positive attitude you'll enjoy finding solutions for your family.

Be confident in the knowledge that the investment of your time in strengthening your family will reap long-term rewards—joy in a loving home.

FAMILY CONTRACT

The _____ family
                    (Write your name here)

wants to find solutions that will strengthen our family.

We commit to spending time together

participating in *Solutions for LDS Families.*

We will meet together and learn the concepts in the lessons.

Our family will participate in the discussions, activities, and assignments.

As we apply these lessons, we can experience greater happiness

and increased love and peace in our home.

Signatures of Family Members

_____   _____

_____   _____

_____   _____

_____   _____

_____   _____

FAMILY HOME EVENING

In February 1999, the First Presidency sent a letter to the membership of the Church throughout the world. The letter included the following instruction:

> We counsel parents and children to give highest priority to family prayer, family home evening, gospel study and instruction, and wholesome family activities. However worthy and appropriate other demands or activities may be, they must not be permitted to displace the divinely-appointed duties that only parents and families can adequately perform (*Ensign*, June 1999, 80).

In addition to receiving the blessings that come from following the prophet, the best way to be organized as a family is to hold weekly family home evenings. By doing this, families enjoy a special closeness and stability. Choosing to spend time with your family sends a message more powerful than words. Memories made together during this time will bond and sustain your family through the years.

Did you know that the counsel to hold regular "home evenings" was given by President Joseph F. Smith as early as 1915? At the time that this instruction was given, the First Presidency issued this promise: "If the Saints obey this counsel, we promise that great blessings will result. Love at home and obedience to parents will increase. Faith will be developed in the hearts of the youth of Israel, and they will gain power to combat the evil influence and temptations which beset them."[4]

Family home evening should be an important part of your weekly schedule. It lends itself well to three parts. These are suggestions only; your family home evening can take any form you wish.

PARTS OF FAMILY HOME EVENING:

1. Family council
2. Lesson
3. Activity

1. Family Council

The family council is a time to do three things: schedule activities, talk about family matters, and plan the next family home evening.

• *Schedule activities.* Coordinating schedules and planning family activities need to be done weekly. When everyone is present (with calendars or note paper), discuss each day of the week. Try to plan a daily schedule that allows your family to eat at least one meal together each day—even if meal time is a little later or earlier than is most convenient for every person. Sometimes individual schedules need to be adjusted for the good of the family.

Talk about upcoming events. Decide when family members can support one another by attending each other's activities. Then plan one family activity. Remember to talk about all the details of the activity. This will include the date, time, meeting place, money and food needed, special clothes to be worn, etc. When conflicts arise, this family activity has highest priority.

- *Talk about family matters.* Discuss household chores, family problems, and anything else a family member wants to talk about.

A family discussion is the core of the family council. This is a valuable opportunity each week to gather around and share feelings about the family. Anything that needs to be discussed can be shared at this time. It is very important that all family members speak only positively and allow the person talking to share his or her feelings in an atmosphere of empathy and caring. This is a time to voice concerns and suggestions for the good of the family.

- *Plan next week's family home evening.* For better assurance that your next family home evening will be successful and that each family member will be involved, talk about who will give the lesson, who will help with the activity, and who will prepare the treats.

2. Lesson

Family home evening is an excellent time to teach a lesson. This can be a discussion on gospel principles, correct behavior, good manners, or one of the important moral values that help shape children's characters. Priceless is the opportunity to meet together regularly as a family and learn the important lessons of life. Parents, this is your stewardship. Unless you teach your children, how will they learn the principles and values you want them to know?

Decide as parents in advance what should be taught each week. A sample lesson on gratitude is included at the end of this section.

3. Activity

The activity is an important part of family home evening. Families need to have fun together! The activity should be something that everyone enjoys. It could be as simple as a family walk in the neighborhood or playing a board game. The activity could be watching a movie as a family, going to a sporting event, or doing service for a friend or neighbor. The most important thing is that the family is all together, enjoying themselves.

As a family, read the following information about family home evening. Then hold your family meeting using as many of the suggestions as possible. Don't be discouraged if your family home evenings aren't perfect—very few are. Do your best and congratulate yourselves on participating in an activity that will bring your family closer together.

SUGGESTIONS FOR FAMILY HOME EVENING

1. Choose a special time each week that you set aside just for the family.

2. Cut out all distractions during that time—no TV, no homework, no phone.

3. Let family members know that this is the family's time for each other.

4. Allow family members to take turns being responsible for parts of the meeting. Family members will feel more involved and will learn more if they participate in the meeting. Children can prepare a poem, story, song, part of the lesson, refreshment, or activity. You may want to rotate the responsibilities of the weekly meeting to involve the entire family.

5. Adapt the lessons and activities to the needs of your family. Every family has different strengths and weaknesses. Think about lessons your family needs and activities your family will enjoy, then plan lessons and activities to meet those needs.

6. Plan fun family activities. Time together should be enjoyable. Playing games, cooking, or giving service are some suggestions for weekly-meeting activities. The possibilities are limited only by your imagination.

7. Keep the tone of the meeting positive. This is a time when each family member should feel loved and accepted. Everyone should be able to speak without being criticized. It can be a time for setting family goals and solving family problems. It should always be a time to enjoy each other. It is most important to be positive and patient.

SAMPLE FAMILY HOME EVENING AGENDA

Welcome _____

Song _____

Prayer_____

Family Council

1. Discuss and schedule the week's activities.

2. Discuss family matters: household chores, family problems, or anything else a family member wants to talk about with the whole family.

3. Plan next week's family home evening.

Lesson _____

Prayer_____

Activity_____

Treats_____

SAMPLE FAMILY HOME EVENING LESSON

Gratitude

Today we're going to talk about gratitude. Gratitude is being thankful for who you are and for things you have.

To begin, let's each name some of the things for which we're grateful.

(The person giving the lesson should now call on one family member at a time and ask them to name two things they're grateful for. Some answers might be, "I'm grateful for our house, for our family, for the gospel of Jesus Christ, for my eyes to see, for my ears to hear, for our dog, for our food, for Grandma, for my teacher, for my friends, etc.)

Sister Geraldine P. Anderson remarked, "There isn't a word in all the English language with more magic in it than the word *gratitude*. Love makes fertile the soil for things to blossom and to grow, and love begins with gratitude" (*Ensign,* Mar. 1971, 53).

Can we be happier if we're grateful for what we have instead of thinking about what we don't have? How can we acquire an attitude of gratitude?

When we wake up in the morning, we can choose to think thoughts of gratitude or of ingratitude. If we have an attitude of gratitude, instead of thinking about the unpleasant things we have to do that day, we'll think of ways to be grateful. We'll think thoughts like, "I'm glad I can get out of bed and walk. I'm grateful that I have food for breakfast, and that I can see this beautiful day. I'm glad I have a place to go today where people need me."

Do thoughts like those help people be happy? Would other people enjoy being around us because of our good attitude?

President Spencer W. Kimball said, "In many countries, the homes are barren and the cupboards bare—no books, no radios, no pictures, no furniture, no fire—while we are housed adequately, clothed warmly, fed extravagantly. Did we show our thanks by the proper devotion on our knees last night and this morning and tomorrow morning?"[5]

Elder Marion G. Romney reminded us, "It is perfectly evident . . . that to thank the Lord in all things is not merely a courtesy, it is a commandment as binding upon us as any other commandment" (*Ensign,* Nov, 1982, 50; see D&C 59:5). President Lorenzo Snow advised, "Always cultivate a spirit of gratitude. It is actually the duty of every Latter-day Saint to cultivate a spirit of gratitude."[6]

I'd like to share with you a poem about gratitude. It's called "The World Is Mine."

THE WORLD IS MINE

Today upon a bus I saw a lovely maid with golden hair;
I envied her—she seemed so gay—and I wished I were as fair.
When suddenly she rose to leave, I saw her hobble down the aisle;
She had one foot and wore a crutch, but as she passed, a smile.
Oh God, forgive me when I whine.
I have two feet; the world is mine!

And then I stopped to buy some sweets.
The lad who sold them had such charm.
I talked with him; he said to me,
"It's nice to talk with folks like you.
You see," he said, "I'm blind."
Oh God, forgive me when I whine.
I have two eyes; the world is mine!

Then walking down the street,
I saw a child with eyes of blue.
He stood and watched the others play;
It seemed he knew not what to do.
I stopped for a moment, then I said,
"Why don't you join the others, dear?"
He looked ahead without a word,
And then I knew he could not hear.
Oh, God, forgive me when I whine.
I have two ears; the world is mine!

With feet to take me where I'd go,
With eyes to see the sunset's glow,
With ears to hear what I would know,
Oh, God, forgive me when I whine.
I'm blessed, indeed! The world is mine!

— Author Unknown[7]

As a family, let's be more grateful each day for who we are and for all we have. Let's each try to keep an attitude of gratitude. (Tell your family how much you love and appreciate each one of them and that you'll do your best to have more gratitude.)

FAMILY MISSION STATEMENT

A family mission statement is like a family constitution. It is a statement of your beliefs and your goals as a family. It is the definition of the course you want your family to take. Once you have that sense of direction, you can set your long- and short-term goals. You will have the vision and values that direct your lives.

Like all families, your family needs to have a clear understanding of where you are going. When you follow a plan, each day will be in harmony with the vision you have of your lives. The steps you take will be in the right direction—toward your personal and family goals.

Define your goals. As a family, decide together what you really want to accomplish. If you don't define your goals, you can get caught up in the busyness of life and forget the things that really matter most to you. A great way to start is to create a family mission statement.

ACTIVITY

Create a family mission statement. It is important that all family members participate. Everyone should think of things they would like to include.

Example of Family Mission Statement:

The _____ family goal is to live together in the celestial kingdom. We will do this by being loving and kind, obeying Heavenly Father's commandments, obeying our family rules, supporting one another, and serving one another. In all of our thoughts, words, and actions, we will try to be loving and kind.

We will obey our family rules.

Our rules are: _____
_____
_____

Our family will support each other in our interests and talents by attending one another's activities. We will give service to one another and to our neighbors. We will always love each other.

Someone in your family might say, "Let's be cheerful," or, "Let's treat each other the way we want to be treated." Anything that the family agrees is a good goal or belief can be added.

Once everyone agrees on the behaviors that are important to your family, write them down. It is your mission statement. Put it up somewhere in your home where it can be easily seen.

Here's one way you can use your mission statement: If, for example, a brother hits his sister, walk over to the family mission statement with him (it will be hanging on the wall) and say, "Look, you signed our family mission statement. It says we all want to love one another, and that means no hitting, doesn't it? Hands are for helping, not hurting, honey. Now, what would you like to say to your sister? And in our family what is the consequence for hitting?"

Through the years and in many ways, our Fellingham family mission statement has blessed our lives. Below is our statement as another example statement.

The Fellingham Family Mission Statement

Our Fellingham family mission is to assist
each family member to attain exaltation in the celestial kingdom.
We will accomplish this by being obedient, kind,
supportive, giving service, and always loving one another.
We will be obedient as we keep our Heavenly Father's commandments,
have family prayer, family scripture reading, and family home evening.
We will obey our family rules.
We will be kind as we ask, "What would Jesus do?"
We will be cheerful, avoiding sarcastic
humor, and speak with a patient tone of voice.
We will treat one another as we would like to be treated.
The Fellingham family will support each other
in our interests and talents by attending one another's activities.
We will give service to each other and to our neighbors.
We will love one another forever and ever, amen.

DISCUSSION

Talk about how a family mission statement contributes to family unity and happiness. Some answers might be, "Having a mission statement in our home will help us act better. Our goals will be on the wall where we can read them often." Or, "With a family mission statement, we'll feel more like a team working together toward family happiness."

ASSIGNMENT

Read your family mission statement regularly. An ideal time to do this is at the beginning of your weekly family meeting, but any time is fine. Talk about how closely your actions match the goals you decided on as a family. Highlight areas of improvement and discuss as a family what is hindering progress.

Chapter 1
Kindness Solution

For the mountains shall depart, and the hills be removed;
but my kindness shall not depart from thee...saith the Lord.
—Isaiah 54:10

Be ye kind one to another.
—Ephesians 4:32

Introduction for Parents

Kindness has been chosen as the first and most important "family solution" because it is a key to individual happiness and family peace. Elder Victor L. Brown remarked, "The measure of a man is not necessarily his title or his position, but rather how he treats others" (*Ensign,* Nov. 1989, 76). Dr. Albert Schweitzer, a well-known humanitarian, once said, "Constant kindness can accomplish much. As the sun makes ice melt, kindness causes misunderstanding, mistrust, and hostility to evaporate."[8]

As I have met with hundreds of families, spoken to numerous groups about family issues, and observed families for decades, I have come to know that kindness is indeed a foundational part of every happy home. Without kindness, the money and the time we give our families are meaningless. Where there is no kindness, all attempts at family solidarity are useless.

Kindness can be shown in many ways, every day. We have countless opportunities to show kindness in the home. I've heard it said in different ways, but the message is always the same: little, frequent acts of kindness are appreciated far more than large material gifts given without affection. Simple words and deeds that show caring and concern for one another should be a part of the fabric of family life. When we treat one another as we would like to be treated, showing kindness, our acts of goodness will be noticed and imitated, creating habits of kindness and traditions of family love.

Parents, I would like to share four ways we can be kind: in our thoughts, words, tone of voice, and actions. These are the four topics of the lessons in this chapter.

First, let's talk about our thoughts. Since our thoughts precede and determine our words and actions, it follows that if our thoughts are kind, our words and actions will also be kind. I believe that the first step in being kind is to think kind thoughts about ourselves. Many times I've heard parents say things like, "I'm not a good mother," or, "I'm always yelling at my kids." Parenting is difficult, and it challenges the abilities of us all. However, we need to be kind to ourselves as we parent by thinking things like, "I may not be doing everything right, but I love my children. I'm trying to learn and improve, and I'm making the best decisions I can." Then if hindsight shows that some of our decisions weren't the best, we can think to ourselves, "I made the best decision I could with the information I had at the time," and get on with life. We should learn from mistakes, not beat ourselves up over them. Let's be kind in our thoughts about ourselves.

Also, we should think kindly of family members. It is easy to be offended and dwell on our unkind thoughts toward others, but unkind thoughts damage souls, tarnish attitudes, and weaken self-images. A better way is to refuse to be offended. Choose to be in control of your own thoughts. Instead of negative thinking, you could think something like, "My son (or any relative) doesn't know how much his remark hurt my feelings. I need to talk to him and let him know how I feel." Then, go to your son and speak kindly and calmly. You could say something like, "Son, when you made that unkind remark, I don't think you knew how much you hurt my feelings. When you said that, how did you want me to feel?" Then, hopefully, your son will think about his remarks and your feelings, and you can discuss them.

A second way we can choose to be kind is by the way we speak. In 1998, President Gordon B. Hinckley asked, "You mothers, are you the kind to scream at your children, shout with shrill voices? Please don't. Be quiet in your talk. Soft words. 'A soft answer taketh away wrath' (Prov. 15:1). It does. Bless your children with the love that you carry in your hearts. 'All thy children shall be taught of the Lord; and great shall be the peace of thy children,' said Isaiah (Isa. 54:13). How true it is. Be teachers to your children" (*Ensign*, Mar. 1999, 72).

Every time we open our mouths to speak, we have choices. We can choose to talk to our children kindly, passively, or unkindly. For example, we can say kindly, "Honey, will you please shut the door?" Or passively we can say, "Shut the door." A third choice may be to shout unkindly, "Shut the door, stupid!" Lesson Ten, Positive Words, offers suggestions of how to change negative statements into positive ones. For years our family had a gold decoration on our door with a motto which read, "Kindness Spoken Here." I enjoyed using it as an expression of one of our family goals.

As parents learn quickly, example is the best teacher—for good and for bad. From their earliest years our children imitate our words and actions. If we want children to speak kindly, we need to speak gently. Praise, compliments, and acknowledgment of their achievements (no matter how small) are music to their ears and food to their souls. Self-images are fragile and need to be handled with kindness. We should speak the way we would like to be spoken to.

Third, let's talk about the tone of voice we use in our homes. Would we speak to our employer or best friend the way we speak to our children? As you will read in Lesson Three, Kind Tone of Voice, many times it isn't *what* is said, but rather *how* it's said that makes people happy or unhappy.

Our voices carry a great deal of power and send messages to those around us. If we want our children to receive a message of love, our tone of voice needs to be kind. When discipline is required, voices can be firm and still send the message, "Even though I dislike what you did, I still love you."

The fourth way we can show kindness is through our actions. They can range from small acts like a smile, a wink, or a touch on the arm to great acts of sacrifice such as donating an organ to someone who needs it to sustain life. For parents, one of the greatest acts of kindness is to give children our time. By doing this we are giving of ourselves in a way that tells children, "My mom (or dad) loves me. See, she wants to be with me—I am important to her!" It is my belief that children are in our homes for such a short time that we should do all we can to create sweet memories.

In addition to showing kindness in the ways listed above, we can sometimes make a special effort to be kind by scheduling acts of kindness individually and as a family. We can set aside a little time on a regular basis—five minutes, fifteen minutes, an hour—whatever we choose, and not let anything interfere. We should treat this time for showing kindness just like any other important scheduled appointment. For example, we can call someone who would like to hear from us, write a letter, or perform an act of service as a family. Anything we do will be showing love and making the world a better place.

Showing Kindness In the Home:

- Demonstrates the care and concern family members feel for one another
- Creates a loving atmosphere
- Prevents problems

We're all happiest when we feel loved—when we know people care about our feelings and have concern for our well-being. Where there is kindness, there is an atmosphere of love, and problems that weaken families are often prevented.

Kindness can be thought of as a circle that can be broken either by failure to show kindness or by failure to receive it. It is equally important both to show kindness and to be able to receive it. Usually we parents are so concerned about teaching children how to give that we don't help them learn how to receive. Parents need to teach children to be gracious and return kindness with expressions of gratitude. For example, thank-you notes sent to gift givers are always appreciated and often result in the givers' desires to give again. Simple smiles and words of appreciation following acts of kindness help keep the "circle of kindness" intact. Russell Lynes said, "The art of acceptance is the art of making someone who has done you a small favor wish that he might have done you a greater one."[9]

You may not believe that your family can generously show kindnesses to one another because perhaps your parents didn't show kindness in your home. This is a challenge. Although you cannot change your past, you do have the power to affect your future, to choose how you think and act. You can choose to begin new traditions of kindness in your home. It will be more difficult if examples of kindness were not part of your heritage, but you can practice kindness in your family and leave a legacy of love for your children and grandchildren.

EXAMPLES OF CHRIST'S KINDNESS FROM THE SCRIPTURES

To teach kindness from the scriptures, we can tell our children many stories showing Christ's kindness. For example, think about the time when Christ heard that His cousin John the Baptist had been brutally murdered. Christ was mourning. He wanted, I'm sure, to be alone, so the scriptures say that He went into the desert. What happened? A multitude of people followed Him. When He saw that He had been followed, did He get annoyed? No. Instead He "was moved with compassion toward them, and he healed their sick. And when it was evening, his disciples came to him, saying, This is a desert place, and the time is now past; send the multitudes away that they may go into the villages, and buy themselves victuals. But Jesus said unto them, They need not depart; give ye them to eat" (Matt. 14:14–16). When the disciples showed Him but five loaves and two fishes, Christ performed a miracle so all could eat. This was truly kindness and compassion.

Another example from Christ's life is when He gathered the children saying, "Suffer the little children to come unto me, and forbid them not: for of such is the kingdom of God" (Mark 10:14). As we teach our children, we should remind them that Jesus especially loves the children.

Listen to His gentle words after raising the dead and healing the sick: "Daughter, be of good comfort; thy faith hath made thee whole" (Matt. 9:22), and "Son, be of good cheer; thy sins be forgiven thee" (Matt. 9:2). How kind He was to His disciples who didn't always seem to "get it." Think about how many questions Christ answered—and always in patience, kindness, and love! (And we think *we* get a lot of questions from *our* children!)

Also in the New Testament, Christ teaches us how to strengthen family relationships by being kind. Let's look at five lessons we can learn from Christ:

1. Show Compassion

When Christ came to Marty and Martha after Lazarus had died, the women were crying, very distraught. What did Jesus do? He wept. He didn't say, "Stop crying. I'm here now, and Lazarus will be fine in a moment . . . just stop crying!" No. He put Himself in their position, with their wants, sadness, needs, and desires, and He wept.

Should we be so hasty with our children, saying things like, "It'll be okay. Be tough. Just stop crying!"? No. Rather, we should sit with them and truly listen with our hearts, expressing our concern for their feelings and sharing our love.

2. Give Our Time To Those We Love

Do you ever remember a time in the scriptures when Christ was in a hurry? He made time for those who needed Him. When people asked Christ questions, often He answered not with a hasty response but rather with a story. He gave His children His time.

3. Listen

Do you ever sense that Heavenly Father and Jesus Christ are *not* there for you? Anytime, day or night, that we choose to draw near unto Them, They will draw near unto us. They're good listeners. Listening sends a clear message: "I care about your feelings. I want to understand. You're important to me." As parents, husbands, wives, friends, sons, and daughters, we need to listen.

4. Adapt Our Messages and Interaction to Fit the Needs of Each Individual Family Member

Did Christ always use the same method of teaching or correcting people? No. He was creative and flexible, always adapting to whomever He was addressing and meeting their individual needs. We need to do likewise with our children. We can notice what works and what doesn't work with each child, and we can ask our children, "Honey, what things can I do to help you feel loved?"

5. Forgive

For me, Christ's last gesture of kindness in mortality is the most impressive. During the time that He was experiencing unimaginable agony and pain, as men were pounding nails through His flesh and His bone, Christ looked at them and said, "Father, forgive them; for they know not what they do" (Luke 23:34). We should try to remember that our children are with us for just a brief moment. They come from a loving Father who entreats us to be kind, loving, and forgiving to His special little friends.

The scriptures are rich with powerful examples from which we can learn to be better parents.

Lesson One
Kind Thoughts

If we have Christlike thoughts in our hearts, Christ's teachings will be reflected naturally in our actions.
—Elder Rex D. Pinegar (*Friend*, June 1992, inside front cover)

CONCEPT

Kind thoughts are pleasant ideas that lift the soul. They always come before kind words and actions. How we think determines how we act.

If we want to become kinder people, the first step is to recognize that kindness, and unkindness, begin in our own minds. We can choose to think good thoughts, no matter what is happening around us.

If we're aware of our thoughts, we can better control our words and actions. We need to be aware of what we're thinking and try to catch ourselves in the act of thinking unkind thoughts. When we notice that our thoughts are unkind, we can say to ourselves, "That wasn't kind." Each time we catch ourselves thinking a negative thought, we should try to replace it with a positive one. That way we can prevent unkindness.

In the October 1999 General Conference, President Boyd K. Packer remarked, "As the years passed I found that, while not easy, I could control my thoughts if I made a place for them to go. You can replace thoughts of temptation, anger, disappointment, or fear with better thoughts—with music" (*Ensign*, Nov. 1999, 24). That's true. Singing or humming is a good way to replace negative thoughts. Another way—if unkind thoughts about someone creep into our minds—is to react kindly by trying to imagine what it would be like to be him; with his life, needs, and desires. We should then think about that person in the same kind way we'd want him to think about us.

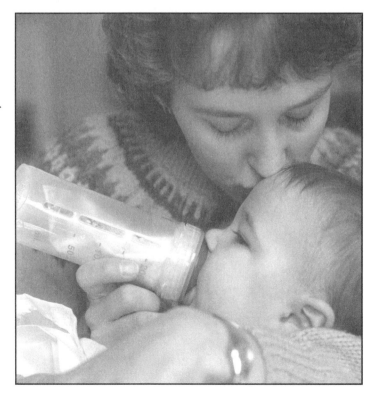

Once we start paying attention to our thoughts, we'll discover that we can better control what we say and how we act. Then we'll be on the road to becoming the kind people we want to be.

President Spencer W. Kimball once asked, "How could a person possibly become what he is *not* thinking? Nor is any thought, when persistently entertained, too small to have its effect."[10] President Ezra Taft Benson explained, "Thoughts lead to acts, acts lead to habits, habits lead to character—and our character will determine our eternal destiny" (*Ensign,* Apr. 1984, 9). Thinking kind thoughts is the first step to living a joyful life.

FAMILY SURVEY REVIEW
Statement 1: Our family thinks kind thoughts about one another.

- Let's name some kind things we can think about each other.
- Give an example of replacing an unkind thought with a kind one.

STORY

Jayne Fisher watched anxiously as her 17-year-old daughter Katie pulled her unruly lamb into the arena of the Madison County Junior Livestock sale. With luck, Katie wouldn't collapse as she had during a livestock show the day before.

Katie was battling cancer. This was her first chance in months to be outdoors having fun, away from hospitals and chemotherapy treatments, and she had come with high hopes for earning some sizable spending money. She had wavered a little on her decision to part with the lamb, but with lamb averaging two dollars a pound, Katie was looking forward to a lot more than a little spending money. So she centered the lamb for viewing, and the bidding began.

That's when Roger Wilson, the auctioneer, had a sudden inspiration that brought some unexpected results. "We sort of let folks know that Katie had a situation that wasn't too pleasant," is how he tells it. He hoped that his introduction would push the bidding up, at least a little bit.

Well, the lamb sold for $11.50 a pound, but things didn't stop there. The buyer paid up, then decided to give the lamb back so that it could be sold again.

That started a chain reaction, with families buying the animal and giving it back, over and over again. When local businesses started buying and returning, the earnings really began to pile up. The first sale is the only one Katie's mom remembers. After that, she was crying too hard as the crowd kept shouting, "Resell! Resell!"

Katie's lamb was sold thirty-six times that day, and the last buyer gave it back for good. Katie ended up with more than $16,000 for a fund to pay her medical expenses—and she still got to keep her famous lamb.

—Rita Price[11]

DISCUSSION

1. Why did the crowd at the livestock sale think kind thoughts about Katie?
2. How did the thoughts of the crowd determine their actions?
3. What can we do when unkind thoughts enter our mind?

ACTIVITY

We're each going to take a turn and share one kind thought about every family member. (One person might say, "Mom is a good cook." The second person might say, "Dad listens to my problems.") One by one, every person in our family will have a turn listening to one kind thought about themselves from each family member.

ASSIGNMENT

Choose one or more of the following:

1. During the coming week make a real effort to have kind thoughts. If you catch yourself thinking an unkind thought, recognize it and replace it with a pleasant thought.

2. Choose one person in the family and try to be very sensitive to his or her feelings for one week. Make a special effort to really feel what that person is feeling and think about them in the same kind way you'd like them to think about you.

3. Participate as a family in the Additional Activity that follows this lesson: Family Time Capsule.

ADDITIONAL ACTIVITY

FAMILY TIME CAPSULE

Most people have strong feelings about what it means to be a member of their family. This activity is an opportunity for family members to share those feelings of why their family is important to them.

ACTIVITY INSTRUCTIONS

1. Give each family member an envelope to hold any of the following:

   • Favorite keepsakes acquired during the past year (awards, letters, etc.)
   • Newspaper clippings, school report cards, original poems, etc.
   • Anything else that represents the person's hobbies or interests
   • Photos of themselves, friends, and activities

2. Give everyone an index card or paper to write down their name, the date, plus any or all the following:

   • Names of friends
   • Something they enjoyed this year
   • Something they want to remember about the year
   • Something they're proud of
   • A goal they have for the next year
   • Advice they'd like to give themselves for the next year

3. Put the card in the envelope.

4. After everyone has filled their envelopes, suggest they write a short note on another piece of paper to each family member for that person to put in their envelope. Notes could include compliments, special memories, or a wish you have for that person.

5. When all of the envelopes have been filled, seal them, put them in the box along with anything else your family would like, and close the box.

6. Write the date on the calendar—in exactly one year—when you will open the box.

In one year open the family box and enjoy your memories.

Lesson Two
Kind Words

We are made kind by being kind.
—Sister Betty Jo Jepson (*Ensign*, Nov. 1990, 91)

FOLLOW-UP

(As a family, discuss the assignment for the lesson "Kind Thoughts.")

1. How are we each doing with recognizing our unkind thoughts and trying to make them more pleasant?
2. Does someone have an experience they would like to share about thinking of others kindly?

CONCEPT

Mother Teresa, well loved throughout the world, once remarked, "Kind words can be short and easy to speak, but their echoes are truly endless."[12] Kind words have the power to heal and to lift. Speaking kindly shows that we care about the person we're talking to. We all feel good when we say kind things to others and when kind things are said to us. On the other hand, when we're spoken to harshly, it is easy to lash back defensively and speak unkindly. Along with harsh words come unpleasant feelings, such as anger, sadness, and regret.

When we speak negatively, it focuses our attention on what is wrong with our world and our circumstances. It doesn't help improve things—it makes our life worse. An unkind remark to another person can range in degree from seemingly harmless to truly hurtful. The truth is, however, whether we're being simply sarcastic or intentionally cruel, the effects are similar. Both types of remarks leave the giver and the receiver feeling negative and critical. President Gordon B. Hinckley taught, "I hope you will not indulge in put-downs, in pessimism, in self-recrimination. Never make

fun at the expense of another. Look for virtue in the lives of all with whom you associate" (*Ensign,* Mar. 1997, 60).

When we speak kindly of others, it focuses our attention on their goodness. When we speak positively of our circumstances, it turns our thoughts toward gratitude for what we have. In 1921, Susa Young Gates said, "Let me whisper this secret in your ear: Every time you try to encourage someone else, your own soul will be flooded with light and glow of peace and good cheer" (*Relief Society Magazine,* Sep. 1921). It's true! All that we send into the lives of others comes back into our own.

Imagine a typical example of how one person could speak kindly to a stranger:

> A gentleman in the grocery store waits at the checkout while a young mother struggles with two children. As the man watches the scene, he notices how incredibly patient the checkout clerk is. The clerk calms the young mother, helps her with her coupons, and even holds the baby while the woman counts her money. After the mother leaves, the gentleman says to the clerk, "I'm so impressed with your patience and kindness with that customer." The clerk looks at him sincerely and says, "Thank you, sir. You are the first customer in eight years to give me a compliment."

How much of a difference do our simple acts of goodness make in the lives of others? And how much brighter are our days when we notice kind acts? We will be delighted to discover that as we begin to notice and acknowledge people's goodness, that is how we'll think of them, and their goodness is what we'll see. We will recognize the beautiful rose instead of the thorn, the glass half full instead of half empty. We will enjoy a dimension of love and gratitude that will spread contagiously to others and help us be a force for good in the world.

FAMILY SURVEY REVIEW
Statement 2: In our family we express love for each other.

- How do we express love for each other in our family?
- What are some of the words we say that show we love each other?

STORY

It was an unseasonably hot day. Everybody, it seemed, was looking for some kind of relief, so an ice-cream store was a natural place to stop.

A little girl, clutching her money tightly, entered the store. Before she could say a word, the store clerk sharply told her to get outside and read the sign on the door, and stay out until she put on some shoes. She left slowly, and a big man followed her out of the store.

He watched as she stood in front of the store and read the sign: No Bare Feet. Tears started rolling down her cheeks as she turned and walked away. Just then the big man called to her. Sitting down on the curb, he took off his size-twelve shoes and set them in front of the girl saying, "Here, you won't be able to walk in these, but if you sort of slide along, you can get your ice-cream cone."

Then he lifted the little girl up and set her feet into the shoes. "Take your time," he said. "I get tired of moving them around, and it'll feel good to just sit here and eat my ice cream." The shining eyes of the little girl could not be missed as she shuffled up to the counter and ordered her ice cream cone.

He was a big man, all right. Big body, big shoes—but most of all, he had a big heart.

—Anonymous[13]

DISCUSSION

1. Why do you think the man in the story gave his shoes to the little girl?
2. Do we sometimes think kind thoughts, but we're too afraid to say them? What are we afraid of?

ACTIVITY

For our activity we're going to read The Power of Appreciation following this lesson, then do one (or more, if you'd like) of the activities included there.

ASSIGNMENT

Choose one or more of the following assignments:

1. With everyone participating, name five kind things you can say to make someone happy.
2. Make a special effort to use kind words in your home.
3. All family members give one compliment each day for a week.

ACTIVITY

THE POWER OF APPRECIATION

One of the important ways to communicate love in families is to express appreciation. We all enjoy being with people who make us feel good about ourselves. Family members who make the effort to notice the good things we do and express their thoughts of appreciation help us feel good. When we feel good about ourselves, it's easier to give to others.

Think of an experience you've had trying to do something nice for someone only to have it go unappreciated. Have you ever expected to hear praise, and instead you were criticized? Let's compare this with an athletic game. Imagine yourself trying to learn a new game. You've been told the rules by an official, and you are now on the field ready to play. The game begins, and you start playing the way you think you're supposed to, when suddenly the official blows the whistle and calls you over. The official explains what you did wrong, which contradicts what you remember being told before the game. He gives you a warning to play by the rules. The action begins again but is stopped almost immediately, and the official scolds you again. Imagine this is repeated each time the game is started. No matter what you do, it's wrong.

You would quickly begin to feel confused and frustrated. Depending on your personality, you might become withdrawn and discouraged, or you might become angry and aggressive at constantly being stopped. You might decide the game isn't worth playing.

Unfortunately, all too often families get into a pattern like this. People are trying their best, but the focus is on what they do wrong rather than on what they do right. We often think that in order for someone to learn or improve, we need to criticize what they did wrong.

Answer three questions:

1. Do we like it when people criticize us?
2. Do we want to share our thoughts and concerns with them?
3. How do we feel about ourselves when we're criticized?

Criticizing others not only creates bad feelings, it isn't a good way to get people to change. It's a fact that animals can be trained much faster if they're rewarded for each correct attempt rather than being punished each time they fail. This principle holds true for people too. We improve our performance faster with praise than with criticism.

It seems to be a law of human behavior that how we act is contagious. In other words, if we are kind to others in our family, we receive kindness in return. Likewise when someone criticizes us, our response tends to be to criticize them in return. In families, it is especially important that we avoid the vicious circle of criticism, which always hurts relationships.

William James, considered by many to be the greatest American psychologist, wrote a book on human needs. Years after the book was published he remarked that he had forgotten to include the most important need of all. He said, "The deepest craving of human nature is the need to feel appreciated."[14] Establish an atmosphere of appreciation in your family by overlooking the negative and "catching" one another doing good things.

Expressing appreciation is not difficult. It requires making the effort to notice the positive things that happen and telling the person involved how you feel about it. If Mom doesn't get a sale she has been working on, other family members can remind her that she got three last week. If a child doesn't do well in one subject, parents can point out his good grades in other areas.

Three Appreciation Activites

Activity 1—Showing Appreciation

Have each family member put their name at the top of a piece of paper. Each one should then pass their paper to the person on their right. The recipient then writes on the bottom of the page something specific the giver has done that they appreciate. The writer then folds the paper over at the bottom to conceal what's written and passes it to the next person. After everyone has their paper back, they can read what others have written. Then taking turns, have everyone say something about your family that they appreciate. Be specific about some behavior rather than the more general "We're nice to each other." An example of a specific behavior may be, "I like it when we go on walks together."

Activity 2—Expressing Affection

Family members, including husbands and wives, often think it is not necessary to say, "You are wonderful!" to each other. Everyone needs to know they are needed, appreciated, respected, and admired. Telling your spouse or other family members why they are important to you is a good way to keep your relationships healthy. The following activity can help you share some of your feelings:

1. Make a list of reasons why you love your spouse or other family members.
2. On each day of a calendar (for a week or a month), write one reason why you appreciate them.
3. Decorate the gift calendar with stickers, pictures, clippings, etc.
4. Give the calendar to your spouse or family member as a way to express your feeling for them.

Activity 3—Noticing Good Qualities

In strong families people truly care about one another's well-being, and they say so. The following activity can help family members notice the good things about each other.

1. Suggest that family members make a real effort to look for things they like about each other. These might be:

- Talents, skills, and achievements
- Qualities and characteristics that make the person special
- Something nice the person said or did

2. Encourage family members to let each other know how they feel by writing short notes about the things they have noticed. Example: "Mom, you made a super dinner! Love, Judy"

3. Put the notes under the person's pillow or in a backpack, lunch bag, desk, etc.

4. Write at least one note to each family member every month.

Lesson Three
Kind Tone of Voice

It seems to me that communication is essentially a matter of talking with one another. Let that talk be quiet, for quiet talk is the language of love. It is the language of peace. It is the language of God. It is when we raise our voices that tiny molehills of difference become mountains of conflict.
—President Gordon B. Hinckley (*Ensign*, Apr. 1984, 76)

FOLLOW-UP

(As a family, discuss the assignment for the lesson "Kind Words.")

1. How are we doing with using kind words in our family?
2. Who can tell us about a compliment they gave, or tell about a compliment received from a family member?

CONCEPT

Many times it isn't what is said, but rather how it's said that makes people happy or unhappy. One way to show kindness is to use a gentle tone of voice when we speak. It takes great effort at times, but speaking kindly can become a habit.

Our voices carry a great deal of power and send messages to those around us. When we speak loudly and harshly, people around us often feel upset. On the other hand, when we speak kindly, we encourage feelings of love, calmness, and respect.

As we speak with gentle tones, we'll discover improved feelings in our home, and we'll help create a loving atmosphere. Additionally, when our voice is controlled, we feel better about ourselves than when we lose control. Because we teach best through our example, those who speak with gentle voices will be pleased to hear others speak that way, too.

Another benefit is that calm voices lead to good behavior. If we want our family to behave with love toward one another, one of the best things we can do is to speak gently—one of the worst things we can do is speak harshly.

In Proverbs 15:1 we read, "A soft answer turneth away wrath." President Harold B. Lee cautioned, "When you raise your voice in anger, the Spirit departs from your home."[15]

Using a kind tone of voice will help prevent family problems, make our home a nice place to be, and deepen the love we feel for one another.

FAMILY SURVEY REVIEW
Statement 3: We use a kind tone of voice when we speak.

- How will speaking kindly in our family make a difference in the atmosphere of our home?
- How can we each improve a little in this area?

STORY

The sun shone fiercely on a hot summer day in Salt Lake City, Utah. There was some problem underneath the street near the home of President George Albert Smith, and several workmen from the city had come to fix it.

The workmen were not very careful with their language. They were swearing and using terrible language as the sun beat down on their backs.

Very few people had air-conditioning in their homes in the late 1940s, so nearly everybody had their windows open, hoping to catch any breeze that might cool them. After a while, the neighbors could hardly stand to listen to the workers' words any longer. One of them walked over to where the workmen were digging and asked them to be more considerate. The neighbor pointed out that the Church President, George Albert Smith, lived nearby—couldn't they show some respect for him and keep quiet, please?

At that, the men let loose with a new string of bad words and spoke even more loudly than before.

Quietly, President Smith scurried around in his kitchen and prepared some ice-cold lemonade. He placed some glasses and the full pitcher on a tray, carried it out to the workmen, and said, "My friends, you look so hot and tired. Why don't you come and sit under my trees here and have a cool drink?"

Their anger gone, the men responded to the kindness with meekness and appreciation. After their pleasant little break, the men went back to their labor and finished their work carefully and quietly.

President George Albert Smith believed in treating others with courtesy regardless of how they treated him. On that hot summer day in Salt Lake City he handled a difficult situation with kindness and great wisdom.

—Susan Arrington Madsen (*Friend*, Oct. 1991, 43)

DISCUSSION

1. What made the workers' anger go away?
2. Does using a kind tone of voice help us have a loving atmosphere in our home?

ACTIVITY

There are five sentences we're going to read out loud together. First we'll say them unkindly, then we'll say the same sentence using a kind tone of voice. (Copy and enlarge this page to make word strips that everyone can read together.)

1. Come to breakfast.
2. We're going to be late.
3. Shut the door.
4. Can you listen to me?
5. I want you to understand.

ASSIGNMENT

During the coming week if you use a harsh tone of voice, immediately repeat what you said using a better tone of voice. You'll be amazed at how soon you can change, until using a kind tone of voice becomes a habit.

For example, parents with young children: If your child yells, "Mama, tie my shoe!" you say, "Tone of voice." Then you speak kindly and say, "Mama, please tie my shoe." Have the child repeat your example exactly. When he has spoken correctly, you exclaim, "Yes! That's the right way to talk!" and give him a hug.

For parents with older children: Speak kindly—be an example to them. When parents speak calmly, they can often diffuse anger. Further, parents shouldn't allow disrespectful, unkind talk in their homes. It is our responsibility to be good examples in teaching children to be kind.

Lesson Four
Kind Actions

Every kind act that we perform for one of our Father's children is but a permanent investment made by us that will bear eternal dividends.

—Elder George Albert Smith (*Conference Report*, Apr. 1914, 13)

FOLLOW-UP

(As a family, discuss the assignment for the lesson "Kind Tone of Voice.")

1. Can anyone remember a time this week when you felt like using an unkind tone of voice but spoke gently instead?
2. How can we make speaking kindly a habit?

CONCEPT

Kind actions are anything we do to make a person's life easier or happier without expecting a reward. Kind actions show concern and caring. When we show kindness in our family, we're helping one another feel loved. When people feel loved, they in turn can more easily show kindness to others.

Elder Jack Goaslind Jr. remarked, "Much of our love is confined to mere lip service and dreams of good deeds accomplished, but true love must be expressed in unselfish acts of kindness that bring others closer to our Heavenly Father" (*Ensign,* May 1981, 60).

Kind actions can be very simple—a smile, a pat on the back, helping with a chore, listening with interest when someone needs you, or doing a job that needs to be done without being told. When family members ask themselves the questions, "What can I do to make another person's life easier?" or, "What can I do to help someone I love?" there are usually countless answers. Being in a family gives us many opportunities to show kindness every day.

Our kind actions come from our thoughts—the desires we have to be good and loving. At the end of each day we should think, "How closely did my actions today match my good intentions to be kind?" Being aware of our actions will help us improve them day by day until we become truly kind in thought, word, and deed.

In general conference of October 1990, Sister Betty Jo Jepsen said, "Kindness has many synonyms—love, service, charity. But I like the word *kindness* because it implies action. It seems like something you and I can do" (*Ensign,* Nov. 1990, 91).

FAMILY SURVEY REVIEW
Statement 4: We treat one another the way we like to be treated.

- Is this true in our family?
- What can we do to live the Golden Rule (Do unto others as you would have others do unto you)? (Suggestions: We can try to understand the other person's feelings before we speak or act. Also, we can ask ourselves the question, "Would I want them to treat me this way?")

STORY

Years ago, at the 1984 U.S. Special Olympics in Seattle, Washington, nine contestants assembled at the starting line for the hundred-yard dash. Every runner was either physically or mentally disabled. At the sound of the gun they all started out, not exactly in a dash, but each with great excitement to run the race to the finish and win.

Suddenly, one boy stumbled on the asphalt and fell. He lay on the ground and cried. When the other contestants heard the boy crying, they slowed down and stopped. Then all eight of those special young people turned around and went back. One girl with Down's syndrome bent down and kissed him, saying, "This will make it better." They picked up their fallen competitor, then all nine linked arms, and, grinning broadly, they walked together to the finish line.

Everyone in the stadium that day was touched by the compassionate act of kindness they had witnessed. The audience unanimously gave the runners a long, enthusiastic standing ovation.

DISCUSSION

1. Do you think each young person wanted to win?
2. When one boy stumbled, what did the runners do?
3. If you were the runner that day, do you think you would have stopped? Why?

ACTIVITY

For our activity, let's each think of a time when someone in our family was kind. The one who begins will explain the kindness that was shown. We won't tell yet who the kind person was. Let the family guess. The one who guesses right is the next one to tell about someone being kind. Each time, the person who showed the kindness is to keep quiet. This is an example of how it will work: One person will say, "Someone made a great dinner for the family tonight. Who is it?" or, "Someone helped me with my homework. Who is it?" If the children are small, Dad may say something like, "Someone ran to the corner to meet me when I got off the bus. Who is it?"

No one gets a second turn until everyone has had one turn. The game can continue as long as everyone wants to play. (If your family is small, acts of kindness by grandparents and friends can be shared.)

ASSIGNMENT

1. Answer these questions:

   • If someone in my family is unkind to me, am I unkind to them to get even?
   • Do my actions show that I love my family?

2. Do at least one kind thing for each family member during the coming week. Anonymous acts of kindness can be even more special.

3. If you wish, read the Additional Solution for Success: Giving and Receiving Affection.

ADDITIONAL SOLUTION FOR SUCCESS

GIVING AND RECEIVING AFFECTION

Some years ago, hospitals and orphanages discovered a fascinating phenomenon known as the "Failure to Thrive" syndrome. Babies who were in the hospital for a long time began to lose weight. They were also not learning to sit up or crawl, and they didn't show any interest in what was going on around them. In some cases, they even died. At first, authorities were very puzzled by the problem. These babies were being cared for physically in every way that was needed. Doctors came to realize that these babies were not receiving enough affection. Nurses were told to hold the babies often and to take time from their duties to talk and sing to the babies. Miraculously, the babies began to grow and progress. Today, most hospitals have a rocking chair in the nursery for nurses and volunteers to hold and rock babies regularly.[16]

None of us really outgrow our need for affection. The outward signs may not be as clear as with small babies, but many people "fail to thrive" because of lack of affection. We all need to receive affection if we are to become the best we can be. We also need to give affection freely so others know we care.

People express affection in different ways. Some are more comfortable than others in giving and receiving affection. For some it is very natural to give kisses, hugs, or pats on the back. For others this can seem awkward. Some people find it easy to speak warmly and affectionately. For others, doing something for someone is their way of showing affection. It should also be remembered that even children from the same family have different personalities and sometimes prefer different expressions of affection.

Family members need to make an effort to show appropriate affection for each other in a sensitive way that allows all family members to feel comfortable. You can determine appropriate ways to show affection to each family member by asking the following questions:

- When you are feeling upset, what can someone do to show they care about you?
- If you have just received an award, how could someone show they are happy for you?
- When you want to show someone you care, would you be more likely to do something special for them, praise them, or give them a hug?

Listen to how everyone answers each question, one question at a time. Differences in the ways people express affection aren't wrong or bad—they are just differences. One of the greatest ways to show people we truly care about them is to accept them the way they are. Acceptance is a great source of support to people. It says to them, "You don't have to change for me. I like you just the way you are."

The giving and receiving of affection in a family is one of the indications of its strength or weakness. Families should give and receive affection freely. The benefits of showing genuine love and kindness to one another will be felt for generations.

SOLUTIONS THROUGH STORIES AND POEMS: KINDNESS

THE BROKEN DOLL

One day my young daughter was late coming home from school. I was both annoyed and worried. When she came through the door I demanded in my upset tone that she explain why she was late. She said, "Mommy, I was walking home with Julie, and halfway home Julie dropped her doll and it broke into lots of little pieces."

"Oh, honey," I replied, "you were late because you helped Julie pick up the pieces of her doll to put them back together."

In her young and innocent voice my daughter said, "No Mommy, I didn't know how to fix the doll. I just stayed to help Julie cry."

—Contributed by Dan Clark[17]

LOVING TIME

A few years ago when I returned to teaching, I was assigned a first grade class. I was a bit apprehensive, since before I had always taught upper grades.

One of my first actions was to eliminate the "Show-and-Tell" period, since I felt that the children who had something to talk about did not require practice in communication, and that the shy ones who needed to speak out were reluctant to do so.

One of the shy ones in this class was a small, curly-headed girl named Teresa. After my announcement Teresa came to me with a request:

"Mrs. Silva, instead of 'Show-and-Tell,' can we have a loving time?"

I was not quite sure what she meant, so I asked her to explain. I hope the years will never allow me to forget her answer: "Every once in a while you could lift us and give us a hug and we could tell you something important. It wouldn't take long." So from that day on, whenever a child needed "loving," he would stand close to my desk and receive a hug, a pat, and a few moments of my undivided attention while he told me something "important." We had such a good class that year . . . it was the year my students taught me.

—Contributed by Myrtle Silva[18]

WHAT IS LOVE?

The story of how Anne Sullivan taught deaf, mute, blind Helen Keller to communicate with others is one of tenderness, courage, and devotion. Helen's perception of the word love is an example.

Miss Sullivan had spelled into Helen's hand, "I love Helen."

"What is love?" Helen asked, but was unable to understand Miss Sullivan's attempt to explain.

A day or two later it had been cloudy, and then suddenly the sun broke forth in warmth.

"Is this not love?" Helen asked.

"Love is something like the clouds that were in the sky before the sun came out," Miss Sullivan replied. "You cannot touch the clouds, you know; but you feel the rain and know how glad the flowers and the thirsty earth are to have it after a hot day. You cannot touch love either; but you feel the sweetness that it pours into everything. Without love you would not be happy or want to play."

"Truth burst upon my mind," Helen wrote later. "I felt that there were invisible lines stretched between my spirit and the spirits of others."

—Adapted from Helen Keller, *The Story of My Life*[19]

THE KING'S HIGHWAY

Once a king had a great highway built for the members of his kingdom. After it was completed, but before it was opened to the public, the king decided to have a contest. He invited as many as desired to participate. Their challenge was to see who could travel the highway best.

On the day of the contest the people came. Some of them had fine chariots, some had fine clothing, fancy jewelry, or great food. Some young men came in only their normal robes, but all ran along the highway. People traveled the highway all day, but each one, when he arrived at the end, complained to the king that there was a large pile of rocks and debris left on the road at one spot, and this got in their way and hindered their travel.

At the end of the day, a lone traveler crossed the finish line and wearily walked over to the king. He was tired and dirty, but he addressed the king with great respect and handed him a bag of gold. He explained, "I stopped along the way to clear away a pile of rocks and debris that was blocking the road. This bag of gold was under it all, and I want you to return it to its rightful owner."

The king replied, "You are the rightful owner."

The traveler replied, "Oh no, this is not mine. I've never known such money."

"Oh yes," said the king, "you've earned this gold, for you won my contest. He who travels the road best is he who makes the road smoother for those who will follow."

—Author Unknown[20]

THE PUPPY

A small boy once inquired about puppies for sale at a home in a well-to-do neighborhood. Noticing that the little one was dressed poorly, the lady of the house replied, "Oh, but they're very expensive—fifteen dollars each."

The boy replied, "I have only two dollars."

"I'm sorry."

"But, I heard there was one with a bad leg. May I look at him?"

"Well, certainly . . . if you wish."

Arriving in the garage, the boy quickly spotted the crippled pup, and picked it up. They immediately stole each other's hearts with natural affection.

"I'd sure like to have this dog, ma'am."

"But surely you don't want a crippled dog."

The little one raised his pant leg to reveal a brace that he had worn since being afflicted with polio, and said, "I think he needs someone who understands him."

The boy returned home that day with a loving pet and two dollars.

—Author Unknown[21]

YOU'RE SO KIND

When I first went to work as a nurse in the old folks' home, they gave me the most difficult cases, and one was an old woman who used to sit in a rocking chair all day long. Nobody liked her. The other nurses avoided her, and that's why I was given the assignment. I thought to myself, "If the Christian message of love means anything, it means something now with this woman." So I pulled up a rocking chair and just rocked alongside this woman and loved her and loved her. The third day she opened her eyes and said, "You're so kind." Those were the first words she had spoken in three years. In two weeks she was healthy enough to be out of the home.

—Author Unknown[22]

THE VALUE OF A SMILE

It costs nothing, but creates much.

It enriches those who receive, without impoverishing those who give.

It happens in a flash, and the memory of it sometimes lasts forever.

None are so rich that they can get along without it, and none are so poor but are richer for its benefits.

It creates happiness in the home, fosters good will in a business, and is the countersign of friends.

It is rest to the weary, daylight to the discouraged, sunshine to the sad, and Nature's best antidote for trouble.

Yet it cannot be bought, begged, borrowed, or stolen, for it is something that is no earthly good to anybody until it is given away!

—Contributed by Dale Carnegie[23]

LESS OF ME

Let me be a little kinder.
Let me be a little blinder
To the faults of those about me.
Let me praise a little more.
Let me be when I am weary
Just a little bit more cheery,
Think a little more of others
And a little less of me.
Let me be a little braver
When temptation bids me waver.
Let me strive a little harder
To be all that I should be.
Let me be a little meeker
With the brother that is weaker.
Let me think more of my neighbor
And a little less of me.

—Contributed by Glen Campbell[24]

I Shall Not Pass Again This Way

The bread that bringeth strength I want to give;
The water pure that bids the thirsty live;
I want to help the fainting day by day;
I'm sure I shall not pass again this way.

I want to give the oil of joy for tears,
The faith to conquer crowding doubts and fears.
Beauty for ashes may I give always;
I'm sure I shall not pass again this way.

I want to give good measure running o'er,
And into angry hearts I want to pour
The answer soft that turneth wrath away;
I'm sure I shall not pass again this way.

I want to give to others hope and faith,
I want to do all that the Master saith;
I want to live aright from day to day;
I'm sure I shall not pass again this way.
                        —Contributed by Ellen H. Underwood[25]

Drop A Pebble in the Water

Drop a pebble in the water; just a splash, and it is gone;
But there's half-a-hundred ripples circling on and on and on,
Spreading, spreading from the center, flowing on out to the sea.
And there is no way of telling where the end is going to be.
Drop a word of cheer and kindness; just a flash and it is gone;
But there's half-a-hundred ripples circling on and on and on,
Bearing hope and joy and comfort on each splashing, dashing wave
Till you wouldn't believe the volume of the one kind word you gave.

Drop a word of cheer and kindness; in a minute you forget;
But there's gladness still a-swelling, and there's joy a-circling yet,
And you've rolled a wave of comfort whose sweet music can be heard
Over miles and miles of water just by dropping one kind word.
                        —Contributed by James W. Foley[26]

Chapter Two
Commitment Solution

I will go and do the things which the Lord hath commanded, for I know that the Lord giveth no commandments unto the children of men, save he shall prepare a way for them that they may accomplish the thing which he commandeth them.

—1 Nephi 3:7

Introduction for Parents

In Rome, Italy, 400 years ago, a sculptor and painter named Michelangelo was on his way to the Sistine Chapel. He was going to work on his ceiling painting for the magnificent church. Only this day was different, because the marvelous painting was nearly complete. It was his final day of work. As Michelangelo slowly climbed up the scaffolding, he could barely see because he was nearly blind from the paint that had dripped down into his eyes as he lay on his back. The great artist Michelangelo had lain on a hard, wood scaffolding, painting a ceiling for seven long years!

As evidenced by the world-famous beauty of the Sistine Chapel ceiling, those who are willing to commit their time and talents to worthwhile causes bring joy into the lives of others. And nurturing children is the ultimate "worthwhile cause."

I'm reminded of the story told by United States president Dwight D. Eisenhower:

> A neighboring farmer had a cow that he wanted to sell. We went over to visit the farmer and asked him about the cow's pedigree. The old farmer didn't know what pedigree meant, so we asked him about the cow's butterfat production. He told us he didn't have any idea what it was. Finally we asked him if he knew how many pounds of milk the cow produced each year. The farmer said, "I don't know. But she's an honest cow, and she'll give you all the milk she has."
>
> I said, "I'm like the cow. I'll give you everything I have."[27]

Can we say, as husbands and wives, as parents, that we're giving everything we have? Are we doing all we can each day to strengthen relationships in our home and bring our children closer to Christ?

It all begins with our own commitment to the Savior. Christ has offered to us His invaluable example, clear commandments to follow, and undeviating direction from prophets through the ages. If we are committed to Him, He will be committed to helping us. In John we learn that after His Resurrection, as He left His Apostles of old, Christ spoke to all of His children, saying, "I will not leave you comfortless"(14:18). "I will pray the Father, and he shall give you another Comforter, that he may abide with you for ever; Even the Spirit of truth; whom the world cannot receive, because it seeth him not, neither knoweth him: but ye know him; for he dwelleth with you, and shall be in you" (John 14:16–17).

Christ, the ultimate teacher, provided us with the Holy Ghost to help us, to guide us, and to be our companion as we learn life lessons during this earthly school.

And what must we do to qualify for the Holy Ghost's constant companionship? We must be truly committed to following the Master, and we must show our commitment through obedience. "If ye love me, keep my commandments" (John 14:15).

I'd like to suggest six ways we can live the virtue of commitment.

1. CREATE A STRONG FAMILY FOUNDATION: A MAGNIFICENT MARRIAGE.

The Great Wall of China was built over many hundreds of years to keep China's northern enemies from invading. The Great Wall was so wide that chariots could ride across the top. It is one of the few man-made objects that astronauts can see from outer space as they look back on the earth. But the Great Wall did *not* keep the enemy out. Do you know why? All the enemy had to do was bribe a gatekeeper. Despite the massive wall, there was an enemy on the *inside* that let in the enemy on the *outside*. So it is in our lives.

Is there an enemy on your inside? What is it? My enemies sometimes change week to week! How about selfishness?

My sweetheart, Gil, has had the opportunity to preside as bishop in five wards and to counsel many couples. He believes that the root of every relationship problem is selfishness.

Is there a tendency in your marriage to think, "Well, I'm doing this for *him,* so he should do this for *me.*"

To eliminate selfishness, we must treat our relationship as a *celestial* marriage. In my mind, *telestial* marriage partners ask, "How can I get more of what I deserve?" They are self-centered. *Terrestrial* marriage partners ask, "How can we set this up so it's fair?" "I washed the dishes last night, so you have to wash them tonight!" or, "He did that to me, so I'm really going to get back at him!" Partners in a *celestial* marriage, on the other hand, ask, "What can I do to help her be happy?" or, "What can I do to make his life easier?" It's loving as Christ loves.

A celestial marriage is one where love sets the tone for resolving disputes and partners use self-discipline and kindness in their interactions. Although it's much easier said than done, maintaining control of our emotions is an obvious "given" in successful conflict resolution. Here are three steps to anger management:

Label it.

As soon as you feel the anger begin to "well up" inside (and we know how this feels), verbalize it. Label it with something like, "I'm starting to get angry," or, "I can feel myself getting angry." Let yourself and everyone within earshot know that your anger is beginning to flare. This is an incredibly important first step that can prevent huge problems.

Separate until in control.

Physically remove yourself, if possible, from the problem or person. For example, if you are in a discussion that becomes heated, just label it: "I'm getting angry. I'm going to cool off outside for a minute," and walk outside. People usually are back in control within just two to five minutes, but inertia is huge, and we often don't have enough self-control to separate ourselves from trouble. If you can't go outside, go to another room, breathe deeply, and think, "It's not like me to lose control because I don't usually lose my temper. I can work this out. I'll think of a solution and stay in control." Think whatever thoughts work to calm you down. Some people sing, and some count. Do whatever works for you.

Focus on solutions.

Don't go backward asking, "Why?" or blaming others in any way. Just move forward and focus on how you can be part of the solution. Offer ideas and *listen* to suggestions with an open mind and heart. Only if you care more about solving the problem than about your ego will you be able to do this. Ask, "How badly do I want peace and loving relationships?"

President Gordon B. Hinckley said,

> "I . . . challenge . . . every woman who is a wife to set the tone of that which is spoken in the home. It was said of old that 'a soft answer turneth away wrath.' (Prov. 15:1) . . . There is so much of argument in the homes of the people. It is so destructive. It is so corrosive. It leads only to bitterness, heartbreak, and tears. How well advised we would be, each of us, when there is tension, when there is friction, when there is affliction, to speak with consoling words in the spirit of meekness" (Ensign, Nov. 1984, 91).

President James E. Faust suggested,

> "A husband should always try to treat his wife with the greatest courtesy and respect, holding her in the highest esteem. He should speak to her in a kind and a soft manner, showing his love by word and deed. As she feels this love and tenderness she will mirror it and return it tenfold" (*Ensign,* May 1998, 37).

Is your enemy a negative tone of voice? President Hinckley reminds us: "We seldom get into trouble when we speak softly. It is only when we raise our voices that the sparks fly and tiny molehills become great mountains of contention. . . . The voice of heaven is a still small voice; likewise, the voice of domestic peace is a quiet voice" (*Ensign,* June 1971, 72).

Is your personal enemy criticism, or nagging? President Spencer W. Kimball talked about this. He remarked, "Ceaseless pinpricking can deflate almost any marriage. Few people have ever changed for the better as a result of constant criticism or nagging. If we are not careful, some of what we offer as 'constructive' criticism is actually destructive."[28]

Is your enemy simply that you're not giving your marriage partner enough of your time? My friends Barbara and Bryce Winkel wrote the book *Isn't It about Time for Your Marriage?* They have wonderful insights about commitment that I'd like to share with you: "The major problem in many marriages today is overcommitment to interests and activities outside of marriage. . . . This . . . is a form of marital suicide. . . . If you are too tired to do anything together, you have no advantage over couples who don't want to do anything together."[29]

I learned a wonderful metaphor for commitment while living in California. I loved the beautiful trees there laden with blossoms and then fruit. I remember the first time I saw an orchard being pruned. I was horrified! What in the world were those men doing cutting the branches of the trees to stubs! How terrible! I learned later that the act of cutting and pruning is the very process that allows the remaining branches to flower and produce larger, better-quality fruit. The Winkels also used this same concept in teaching about how to discipline ourselves in our commitments.

The Winkels write,

> In a similar way, life offers many opportunities for our talents and interests to branch out. The wise person prioritizes his life and prunes some of his lower-priority interests. This might mean pruning some interests that are worthwhile and enjoyable. . . . We must learn to "just say no" to some lower-priority requests for our time. Remember to

smile when saying "no," because in reality, you are saying "yes" to something else of higher priority.[30]

So ask yourself right now, "What activity am I engaged in that competes with my marriage because it takes too much time?" (Raising children doesn't count!) If you find other things are taking priority, consider this final suggestion from Brother and Sister Winkel:

> Approach it with the same discipline you use to follow a healthy diet. You choose not to eat or drink certain things because you know they're not good for your body. Likewise, cut certain activities from your life because they're in competition with your marriage, and not as important. You may have convinced yourself that you "have to" work late, or play golf, or attend professional organizations, or be on the PTA board, etc. But the truth is, you choose to do these things, and you have the same freedom to choose not to do them. . . .
>
> Look those outside commitments squarely in the eye. Compare the time you invest in them [against] the same amount of time invested in your marriage. Do they have the potential to bring you the same long-term return? If not, prune away!"[31]

Another thought about making a magnificent marriage: Ask yourself these questions: "Do I spend enough time thinking about what I can do to contribute to a great marriage? Do I ever ask my sweetheart what he (or she) thinks I should do to be a better mate?"

Brother Brent Barlow [a professor at BYU] posed a question to a group of priesthood brethren: "How many of you would like to receive a revelation?" Every hand went up. He then suggested they all go home and ask their wives how they could be better husbands. He added, "I followed my own advice and had a very informative discussion with [my wife] Susan for more than an hour that afternoon (*Ensign*, Sep. 1992, 17).

2. Fathers, preside honorably at home, and mothers, exemplify goodness and stay at home to raise the children whenever possible.

The Quorum of the Twelve Apostles issued a statement in 1973 on fatherhood:

> Fatherhood is leadership, the most important kind of leadership. It has always been so; it always will be so. Father, with the assistance and counsel and encouragement of your eternal companion, you preside in the home. It is not a matter of whether you are the most worthy or best qualified, but it is a matter of law and appointment. You preside at the meal table, at family prayer. You preside at family home evening; and, as guided by the Spirit of the Lord, you see that your children are taught correct principles. It is your place to give direction relating to all of family life. You give fathers' blessings. You take an active part in establishing family rules and discipline. As a leader in your home you plan and sacrifice to achieve the blessing of a unified and happy family. To do all of this requires that you live a family-centered life (reprinted in *Ensign,* June 2002, 16).

Elder N. Eldon Tanner taught,

> A mother has far greater influence on her children than anyone else, and she must realize that every word she speaks, every act, every response, her attitude, even her appearance and manner of dress affect the lives of her children and the whole family. It is while the child is in the home that he gains from his mother the attitudes, hopes, and beliefs that will determine the kind of life he will live and the contribution he will make to society (*New Era,* Jan. 1977, 33).

Also, President Ezra Taft Benson remarked, "A mother's role is also God-ordained. Mothers are to conceive, bear, nourish, love, and train. They are to be helpmates and are to counsel with their husbands. There is no inequality between the sexes in God's plan. It is a matter of division of responsibility" (*Ensign,* May 1984, 6).

Another way women can live this virtue of commitment is to obey President Hinckley's teaching for mothers to stay home with their children whenever possible. Obedience or disobedience to that counsel is an indication of our commitment to our family and to the Lord (unless the money the wife earns is required to sustain life). There is no substitute for a child's mother. No one can take her place, no matter who they are or how hard they try. That which a woman forfeits in terms of money or status because she doesn't work outside the home is a small price to pay for obeying the prophet and being a "full-time nurturer." Children are home for such a short time. I know that making the choice to be with them during the years when they need you is a choice you'll never regret.

3. STUDY AND PRAY ABOUT YOUR STEWARDSHIP IN YOUR MARRIAGE AND AS A PARENT.

It amazes me that we spend years studying academic subjects and virtually no time at all studying how to strengthen relationships at home. Take advantage of the wonderful resources available—books written by brilliant men and women who spend their lives researching and learning ways to help people improve their marriages and their parenting skills. Bookstore shelves are lined with books by our Church leaders; take advantage of their efforts by reading and learning what works.

Since example and habit are incredibly powerful, we usually use the same parenting techniques *our* parents used, even if they weren't very effective, and even when we don't agree with their methods!

Take all that was good and wholesome from your past, and leave the negative behaviors behind. If you had less-than-desirable examples, discover *better* ways to parent—to communicate, discipline, etc. Excellence in any field demands study, conscious effort, and usually lots of prayer. Certainly, parenthood should require no less.

4. GIVE YOUR FAMILY YOUR TIME.

When we love and value something, we spend time on it. We can tell what we truly value by how much time we invest in it. For example, a person who loves to golf, garden, fish, read, or scrapbook somehow makes the time to do these things. If you truly value your family relationships, you'll somehow find the time to nurture them.

We should give our children both quality *and* quantity time. Years ago I heard President Ezra Taft Benson give wonderful advice relative to time spent with our children. He counseled, "Be there at the crossroads. . . . take time to always be at the crossroads when your children are either coming or going—when they leave and return from dates, when they bring friends home. Be there at the crossroads whether your children are six or sixteen."[32] As often as possible we need to be there—moms *and* dads—when our children hit their first home run, participate in the school play, graduate, etc. We also need to be there for the less-dramatic times—like when our teenagers need to talk (usually late at night). Time is precious. Time is what lives are made of. We need to be so committed to our children that we are willing to give them our time when we're at our best and not in a hurry. Children don't thrive on "leftover time" as well as on "prime time."

When we are truly committed to our families' happiness and well-being, we'll give them our time and our hearts naturally, without resentment or complaining, because we want to. We won't have to think about it; it'll be part of who we are.

Years ago President Ezra Taft Benson counseled, "Mothers [and fathers], take time to be a real friend to your children. Listen to your children, really listen. Talk with them, laugh and joke with them, sing with them, play with them, cry with them, hug them, honestly praise them" (*Ensign,* May 1987, 97). And Elder L. Tom Perry voiced the feelings of many older parents when he said, "If I were cast again in the role of having a young family around me, I would be determined to give them more time" (*Ensign,* Nov. 1980, 9).

This delightful story explains it well. It's called "When Mother Came to Tea."

> I had no idea she would be there. My apologies for her absence had been well-rehearsed. When my high school home economics teacher announced that we would be having a formal mother-daughter tea, I felt certain I would not be serving my mother at this special event. So I will never forget walking into the gaily decorated gym—and there she was! As I looked at her, sitting calmly and smiling, I imagined all the arrangements this remarkable woman must have had to make to be able to be with me for that one hour. Who was looking after Granny? She was bedridden following a stroke, and Mom had to do everything for her. My three little sisters would be home from school before Mom got there. Who would greet them and look at their papers?
>
> How did she get here? We didn't own a car, and she could not afford a taxi. It was a long walk to get the bus, plus at least five more blocks to the school. And the pretty dress she was wearing, red with tiny white flowers, was just right for the tea. It brought out the silver beginning to show in her dark hair. There was no money for extra clothes, and I knew she had gone into debt again at our coal company store to have it.
>
> I was so proud! I served her tea with a happy, thankful heart, and introduced her boldly to the group when our turn came. I sat with my mother that day, just like the rest of the class, and that was very important to me. The look of love in her eyes told me she understood. I have never forgotten. One of the promises I made to myself and to my children, as young mothers make promises, was that I would always be there for them. That promise is difficult to keep in today's busy world. But I have an example before me that puts any lame excuses to rest. I just recall again when Mother came to tea.
>
> —Contributed by Margie M. Coburn[33]

5. LET OUR CHILDREN KNOW WE'RE TRULY INTERESTED IN THEIR LIVES.

Children know when we're faking it. To convince a child, especially a teenager, that we're interested in every part of his life, we truly have to be interested in every part of his life. To do this, first try and remember what it was like to be young. When your children talk to you, try thinking like a teenager, or a nine year old—whatever age the child is. We should carefully think, "What it would be like to *be* this child, with their life experiences, needs, and desires?" Then we have a better chance of really understanding how he feels so we can empathize with him and help him more effectively.

I have no doubt that my sons, Danny and David, know I was sincerely interested in and supportive of their high school swimming careers. I rode on the bus, with the team, and only missed one meet in six years. My husband, a BYU professor, not only attended every meet, he became certified as an official so he could officiate as a stroke-and-turn judge.

How about our little children? You've probably experienced times like the day my nine-year-old Benjamin came home from school and told me that he felt embarrassed at recess because he missed a soccer goal. The big sixth-grade boys had laughed at him. For just a moment before I responded, I tried to *be* my little Benjamin. I imagined being a three-and-a-half-foot tall fourth grader with older boys laughing and pointing at me in ridicule. I knelt down beside my son and gave him the hug he so desperately needed.

Of course, there are times when we just can't be there when our children need us. But through the years they learn that those times are the exception, not the rule.

6. LET FAMILY MEMBERS KNOW, WITHOUT A DOUBT, THAT WE LOVE THEM.

During the years I was a schoolteacher I taught over three thousand students. Countless times I would see children who would struggle to achieve, fully believing that their parents' love for them was conditional upon their success in school. At first I thought the students were mistaken. Surely parents wouldn't withdraw their love if their child, in spite of his best efforts, did poorly in the classroom. Sadly, too often I was the one mistaken. There were many parents who saw their child's performance at school as a reflection on them and treated the child unkindly when he didn't meet their expectations. These parents gave love only when grades were high, contests were won, and rules were obeyed.

Our children need to know that they are loved regardless of whether they win the game or get good grades. We need to make it very clear to one another that there is nothing we must do to *earn* love. Because we are children of our Heavenly Father, who sent us down to live as a family and sent His Son to teach us how to love, we should love one another!

We need to look in our children's, our parents', and our spouses' eyes and say, "I love you." Often! And we should show our love and our commitment to their eternal happiness through daily acts of kindness.

In October 1995 General Conference, President Gordon B. Hinckley counseled, "You parents, love your children. Cherish them. They are so precious. They are so very, very important. They are the future. You need more than your own wisdom in rearing them. You need the help of the Lord. Pray for that help and follow the inspiration which you receive" (*Ensign*, Nov. 1995, 89).

During our lifetime we make many commitments. We commit to being educated and to attend school. We commit our loyalty to friends. We commit to bank loan officers, employers, and politicians. However, of all the commitments we make in life, commitments to our

Heavenly Father and to our families are the most important. What does being committed to our family mean? I believe it means that we give our hearts and our time to our family, no matter what the consequences may be. We commit to do *whatever is needed* to ensure family happiness in this life and eternal exaltation in the life to come.

Lesson Five
Commit Your Time

One of the main problems in families today is that we spend less and less time together. Some spend an extraordinary amount of time, when they are together, in front of the television, which robs them of personal time for reinforcing feelings of self-worth. Time together is precious time—time needed to talk, to listen, to encourage, and to show how to do things. Less time together can result in loneliness, which may produce inner feelings of being unsupported, untreasured, and inadequate.

—President James E. Faust (*Ensign*, May 1983, 41)

FOLLOW-UP

(As a family, discuss the assignment for the lesson "Kind Actions.")

1. What are some of the ways we are showing more kindness in our family?
2. Can someone share an experience he or she had obeying the Golden Rule (Do unto others as you would have others do unto you)?

CONCEPT

A garden grows well when someone spends time watering and cultivating it. Just like a garden, our family needs us to give our time and effort for it to be successful. Although our jobs, school, and hobbies are important, our family should be the first priority in our lives. We should be willing to give our family both quality and quantity time.

Quality time means that when we are with one another we are 100 percent "there," focused on family members' needs and happiness. Quantity time means that we are with our families as often as we can be. This is a chal-

lenge sometimes, but when family relationships are truly our highest priority, time needs to be given to those relationships. There is no substitute for unhurried time with our loved ones.

When a person comes to the end of his life, he wouldn't reflect on his life saying, "I wish I had spent more time in the office." Relationships are the most valuable thing we have in life, and they are built on time spent together. Time is precious. It is what lives are made of. Giving our time and hearts to our family shows our love for them.

Occasionally, we need to evaluate ourselves and ask the question, "Do my actions reflect a deep commitment to my family?" Elder Richard G. Scott, speaking of creating an ideal family, counseled, "If it requires fundamental changes in your personal life, make them . . . If you have lost the vision of eternal marriage, rekindle it. If your dream requires patience, give it. . . . Don't become overanxious. Do the best you can. . . . Do not be discouraged. Living a pattern of life as close as possible to the ideal will provide much happiness, great satisfaction, and impressive growth while here on earth regardless of your current life circumstances" (*Ensign,* May 2001, 7).

Let's use our precious time to love and lift one another. Elder Hans B. Ringger reminds us, "It takes time to listen and to comfort, it takes time to teach and to encourage, and it takes time to feed and to clothe. We all have the gift to lift each other's burdens and to make a difference in somebody's life" (*Ensign,* May 1990, 26).

Families are like teams—they work together to reach the same goals. Both parents and children have very important positions on the team, and everyone is needed to make it work well. What happens to an athletic team when they don't work together? Usually they don't win. On the other hand, individual players on winning teams are committed to the success of the whole team. They give of themselves, they support and help one another, and they usually do it enthusiastically. Those are also good ingredients for a family. As we commit our time and hearts to our family, we can reach our goals and "win" in the game of life.

FAMILY SURVEY REVIEW:
Statement 5: We enjoy doing things together as a family.

- How can we make our family activities more fun?
- Ask yourself silently, "Can I improve my attitude or my support of family activities?"

STORY
Relate this fictionalized story to open a family discussion:

Little Kevin ran happily to greet his father when he came home from work. Cheerfully, Kevin exclaimed, "Daddy, I've been waiting for you! I wanted you to come home and read this to me!" Kevin held his book up as high as he could, showing it to his father.

John answered his son tiredly, "Yes, I'll read the book to you after dinner."

After dinner John received a telephone call and waved Kevin away with annoyance when Kevin reminded him about the book. After the little boy's bath he found his dad, who had just sat down to enjoy the evening newspaper. "Daddy, when you finish reading your paper, can you read my book to me?"

"Sure, Kevin," was John's reply as he kept his eyes on the newspaper.

An hour later John remembered his promise to Kevin and hurried up the stairs to his son's room. John found the little boy fast asleep with tear-stained cheeks. Kevin's unread book was lying open across his small chest.

DISCUSSION

1. What should the father in the story have done differently?
2. Children, do you ever want your family to spend more time with you?
3. What can we do to give more time to our family?

ACTIVITY

For our activity, let's each think of one thing we would really enjoy doing as a family. Let's make a list of all the fun activities we can think of. Now let's decide on one family activity we will do soon. We'll put it on the calendar and plan how to do it. All of us can help with the planning and preparations. Then let's *do* our family activity.

ASSIGNMENT

Participate as a family in the three Additional Activities that follow this lesson:

1. Our Family Time
2. The Gift of Time
3. Family Dates

ADDITIONAL ACTIVITIES
FAMILY TIME

Strong families enjoy being together, and they make the effort to plan activities to be with one another. Family time doesn't have to be elaborate or expensive. The simplest activities often become the most memorable. Family time can be as simple as sharing a family joke or enjoying a favorite tradition, such as Saturday morning pancakes or a family walk on Sunday afternoons.

Often when children are asked, "What makes a happy family?" they answer, "Doing things together!" It may seem so obvious that it gets overlooked, but doing things together as a family builds family unity.

Sometimes it's difficult for family members to find the time for family togetherness with work, school, Church, and community responsibilities. But the real test of our commitment to our family is the amount of time we spend together. We may have heard that it is quality, not quantity, time spent with children that is important. Since time is at a premium, it *is* important to spend family "quality time." However, it's also important to spend quantities of time in order to create close relationships with family members. Usually when family members spend time with one another they feel more comfortable sharing their deepest feelings.

ADDITIONAL ACTIVITY 1—OUR FAMILY TIME

To begin investing more time together as a family, it's helpful to assess how we now spend our time. We can then decide if that's the way we want to live our lives.

- Take a paper plate and draw lines to divide it into twenty-four pie-piece-shaped sections for the hours of the day. (Divide the plate into thirds, then each third into halves, then each half into fourths. That makes twenty-four sections.)
- Write in the things that absolutely must happen every day. What are those? (Eating, sleeping, working, going to school, etc.) Now write in the other things we do each day.

Ask the following questions:

1. Are we spending our time as we wish?
2. How would we like to spend our time?
3. What is preventing us from spending our time as we want?
4. What can we change so that we can spend our time as we would like to? (Concentrate on the things we can change.)

Ideas for maximizing time together:

- Eat at least one meal together as a family every day.
- Take up an exercise that can be shared as a family.

- Work together on household chores rather than assigning separate tasks to each family member.
- Make community service something that will involve several family members, such as coaching a team or being a club leader.
- Turn off the television and play a game. If you are watching television, discuss the program together.
- Sit by children while they eat breakfast, even if not eating at the same time.
- Develop the habit of chatting with one another while preparing or cleaning up meals.

Family vacations can be special times, especially if everyone is involved in the planning and preparation. From planning the vacation to reliving it with pictures and mementos, a family vacation can be an opportunity to reinforce relationships with family members.

A few years from now as we reflect back on the good times with our families, the time we spent together will probably mean more than the remodeled room or new furniture we worked two jobs to be able to afford. Spending time with your family isn't a luxury—it's a necessity.

ADDITIONAL ACTIVITY 2—THE GIFT OF TIME

One of the ways we show affection and appreciation is by doing things for people. We also show we care about others by spending time with them. The following activity can help you give your family the gift of time.

1. Decide on something special you will do for someone in your family. For example:

- Lunch or dinner date
- Car wash
- Laundry, homework, yard work, etc.
- Ice-cream cone treat
- Movie or video "date"

2. Decide how often you want to give the "gift" (monthly, weekly, etc.).

3. Make a "credit card" issued in the name of the family member, with a description of your gift. Put a space for them to sign it.

4. Mail it to them in the same way they would receive a new credit card.

5. Punch or mark the card each time it is used. Make sure the credit card is used and enjoyed.

ADDITIONAL ACTIVITY 3—FAMILY DATES

One of the best gifts we can give our family is time spent together. That does not mean we must do everything with *all* members of the family. In fact, many times the best "togetherness" is the kind shared one-on-one between parent and child. Finding this time takes planning. This activity can help parents and children make spending time together a priority. Here are some ideas:

- At the start of each month, parents and children schedule a date for spending one-on-one time with each other. If desired, make a family date plan (like the one below) to help organize the dates.
- Mark all family dates on the calendar. Only emergencies can interfere with these dates.
- In two-parent families, Mom and Dad can schedule dates with each other, as well as with the children.

Family Date Plan for _____ and _____
　　　　　　　　　　　　　　　　　(parent)　　　　　　　　　(child)

Activity	Length of Activity	Supplies we will need	Cost

Lesson Six
Goals

Write down your goals and what you plan to do to achieve them.
Aim high, for you are capable of eternal blessings.
—President Thomas S. Monson (*Ensign*, May 1999, 97)

FOLLOW-UP

(As a family, discuss the assignment for the lesson "Commit Your Time.")

1. What are we doing to give our family more of our time?
2. How are our attitudes during family activities?

CONCEPT

A goal is an objective we're trying to reach. Jim Rohn said, "The future does not get better by hope, it gets better by plan. And to plan for the future we need goals."[34] The purpose of goals is to focus our attention on what we want to achieve. We can achieve more individually, and as a family, with clear objectives.

The great basketball player Michael Jordan said, "I visualized where I wanted to be, what kind of player I wanted to become. I knew exactly where I wanted to go and I focused on getting there."[35]

Helmut Schmidt remarked, "The tragedy in life doesn't lie in not reaching your goal. The tragedy lies in having no goal to reach. It isn't a calamity to die with dreams unfulfilled, but it is a calamity to not dream. It is not a disgrace not to reach the stars, but it is a disgrace to have no stars to reach for. Not failure, but low aim is sin."[36]

Elder M. Russell Ballard counseled us, "Set goals that are well balanced—not too many nor too few, and not too high nor too low. Write down your attainable goals and work on them according to their importance. Pray for divine guidance in your goal setting" (*Ensign*, May 1987, 14).

It is encouraging to realize that at any time we can set new

goals for ourselves to improve as individuals and as a family. However, Elder Neal A. Maxwell cautioned us when he said, "The scriptural advice, 'Do not run faster or labor more than you have strength' (D&C 10:4) suggests paced progress, much as God used seven creative periods in preparing man and this earth" (*Ensign,* Nov. 1976, 10–11). Former general president of the Relief Society, Barbara B. Smith, agreed when she said, "Goals are stars to steer by, not sticks to beat yourself with."[37]

FAMILY SURVEY REVIEW:
Statement 6: We set family goals together.

- How can goals help point us in the direction we want to go as a family?
- How can we help one another reach our goals?

STORY

There was once a farmer who hired a teenage boy to help him do the fall plowing. The boy's first day on the tractor was disastrous. Because he was looking backward, watching the plow turn the soil behind him, the boy didn't realize until he reached the end of the field that the row was very crooked.

Toward the end of the day the farmer arrived to survey the young man's work. The crooked rows prompted him to give the boy some advice: "You can't plow a straight row if you keep looking back. You must focus your eyes on a goal straight ahead and move forward toward it—not swerving to the right or to the left—and never look behind you."[38]

President Howard W. Hunter remarked,

To dig a straight furrow, the plowman needs to keep his eyes on a fixed point ahead of him. That keeps him on a true course. If, however, he happens to look back to see where he has been, his chances of straying are increased. The results are crooked and irregular furrows. . . . Fix your attention on your . . . goal[s] and never look back on your earlier problems . . . If our energies are focused not behind us but ahead of us—on eternal life and the joy of salvation—we assuredly will obtain it (*Ensign,* May 1987, 17).

DISCUSSION

1. What is the advice the farmer gave to the teenager?
2. What can we do to keep focused on our goals, as Michael Jordan and the farmer in the story suggested?

ACTIVITY

We're now going to have each family member choose four goals—one in each of four areas: physical, mental, social, and spiritual. Then we'll each list one way to reach our goals. Example:
1. Physical goal: I want to be stronger. I will lift weights three times a week.
2. Mental goal: I want to be smarter. I will read one book each month.

3. Social goal: I want to be well liked. I will be kinder to others.
4. Spiritual goal: I want to feel closer to my Heavenly Father. I will pray and read the scriptures every day.

Now we'll set one family goal. Everyone needs to participate and share their ideas about what our goal should be. Here are four examples:

1. For one week we'll try not to criticize any family member or friend.
2. We will try to be better neighbors by being friendlier and more helpful.
3. Our family will try for one month to exercise more regularly and eat more healthful foods.
4. Our family will read the Book of Mormon this year.

ASSIGNMENT

1. Discuss and plan ways you can help each other reach your goals. Then, during family home evenings, talk about the progress you've made toward your goals. After reaching your goals, congratulate and reward yourselves. Then it's time to set new ones and continue improving your lives.

2. If you wish, read the Additional Solution for Success: Are We Going Where We Think We Are?

ADDITIONAL SOLUTION FOR SUCCESS
ARE WE GOING WHERE WE THINK WE ARE?

Sometimes people spend their resources of time or money on things that bring the least reward in terms of what they really value. Families need to regularly review their goals of how they want to spend their time. Then they need to see if they actually are spending time doing things that bring them lasting joy. If they aren't happy, they need to reevaluate their priorities and actions and have the courage to make changes. If they don't, they may climb the ladder of success only to find that it's leaning against the wrong wall. Too late, families may regret how they spent the years they had together.

To help your family examine what you value most, name things you enjoy doing as a family. Now talk about how often you do the things you really enjoy. Answer these questions:

1. What does our list of things we enjoy doing tell us about what we value most?

2. What does how often we do these things tell us about our priorities?

Despite what you *say*, what you *do* shows how you really feel. What you spend your time doing will show what you really want for your family.

Decide as a family to spend more time doing the things that will strengthen you and make you happy. The following activity will help you look to the future.

ACTIVITY

1. Have one person keep time while everyone writes their answers on paper.
2. Everyone answer the following question in three minutes: "How do you want to spend the rest of your life?" Make a list of goals and activities.
3. Answer the second question in three minutes: "What do you want to do in the next five years?" Again, list goals and activities.
4. Answer the third question in three minutes: "If you only had six months to live, how would you spend it?" List activities and goals.
5. Share one another's ideas and talk about how you can help each other reach your goals.

Lesson Seven
Service

God does notice us, and He watches over us. But it is usually through another person that He meets our needs.
—President Spencer W. Kimball (*Ensign,* Dec. 1974, 5)

FOLLOW-UP

(As a family, discuss the assignment for the lesson "Goals.")

1. What are the goals we set as a family?
2. What are we doing to reach our goals?

CONCEPT

Service is kindness in action. Service is giving to others—lifting loads and brightening lives. Having an attitude of service means looking for ways to help rather than waiting to be asked. The needs of others are important to those who serve unselfishly. They help people because they care about them, not because they expect a reward. Those who serve others will also benefit—they'll enjoy good feelings of self-worth and an increased capacity to love.

Elder Joseph B. Wirthlin remarked, "The temporal and the spiritual are linked inseparably. As we give of our time, talents, and resources to tend the needs of the sick, offer food to the hungry, and teach the dependent to stand on their own, we enrich ourselves spiritually beyond our ability to comprehend" (*Ensign,* May 1999, 76–77).

President Spencer W. Kimball further explained this when he said, "It is by serving that we learn how to serve. When we are engaged in the service of our fellowmen, not only do our deeds assist them, but we put our own problems in a fresher perspective. When we concern ourselves more with others, there is less time to be concerned with ourselves. In the midst of the miracle of serving, there is the promise of Jesus, that by losing ourselves, we find ourselves"(*Ensign,* Dec. 1974, 2).

For children, serving others can be as simple as being friendly at school. One teacher said, "Children who have attitudes of service are alert to situations in which classmates are hurting. If they see a student eating alone, they sit with him. They are understanding and caring."

Elder Russell C. Taylor reminds us of Christ's perfect example: "Jesus washed the feet of his disciples, feet that were hot, sweaty, and soiled with dust and dirt. He washed not their hands or face; he washed their feet. He who is the greatest shall be the least—he it is who learns to serve" (*Ensign*, Nov. 1984, 23).

The truth is that self-centered people are not as happy as those who are "others-centered." Instead of looking at mirrors to see what we need, let's look through windows to see other people's needs. In families and in the Church there are countless opportunities to serve one another.

Elder J. Richard Clarke told this story:

> A dear sister had been incapacitated for the past eight years—she could not walk or talk and was confined to bed. About six years ago, she and her husband were assigned a faithful home teacher. He asked if his wife could come over to their house every Sunday morning and stay with the invalid woman while her husband attended priesthood meeting. For six years, every Sunday this home teacher would bring his wife over to stay with the invalid sister while her husband went to his meeting. And every Sunday the home teacher's wife would bring with her some baked goods or something special that she had made for this older couple.

> Finally, this sister who had been ill passed away. When her daughter tried to express her deep love and appreciation to this loving home teacher and his wife for what they had done over the years, the wife said, "Oh, don't thank us. It was our privilege to visit with your sweet mother. What am I going to do now? The hour and a half on Sunday morning will now be, for me, the loneliest hour and a half in the week" (*Ensign*, Nov. 1981, 79).

Elder David B. Haight reflected, "As I get older and as I look back upon the world and upon the life that I have lived, I sense that it is the love that we share and the service that we render that really is the great payoff" (*Ensign*, May 1999, 68).

FAMILY SURVEY REVIEW
Statement 7: Our family helps one another without being asked.

- Do we help one another? What are some of the things we can do in our family to help each other?
- What are some of the ways we can give service without being asked?

STORY

There are two seas in Israel. One sea, the Galilee, is fresh. Fish live in it. Trees and bushes grow near it. Children splash and play in it. The river Jordan flows into this sea from the north with sparkling water from the hills. People build their homes near it.

Every kind of life is happier because it is there. The same river Jordan flows south out of it into another sea. Here there are no fish, no green things, no homes being built. Stale air hangs above its waters, and neither man nor beast will drink of it. What makes the difference between these neighbor seas? Not the Jordan River. It empties the same good water into both. Nor is it the soil or the countryside.

The difference is that the Sea of Galilee receives water but does not keep it. For every drop that flows in, another drop flows out. The giving and the receiving go on in equal measure. The other sea hoards its income. Every drop it gets, it keeps. The Sea of Galilee gives and gives. The other sea gives nothing. It is called the Dead Sea.

There are also two kinds of people in this world: those Dead Sea–like people who take without giving back, and the givers who remain fresh and vibrant by freely giving service and sharing of themselves.[39]

Discussion

1. Which sea are we like—the Dead Sea or the Sea of Galilee?
2. How can we be more like the Sea of Galilee, giving of ourselves to others?

Activity

As a family, let's participate in one of the acts of service listed below or think of our own:

- Plant a tree.
- Clean/rake/shovel the snow from a neighbor's yard.
- Be friendlier at school.
- Help an elderly person with housework or yard work.
- Tend children for a young mother, without pay.
- Read to a child.
- Pick up trash along the highway.
- Do volunteer work in the community.
- Take a meal to a needy family.
- Contribute to Church and community projects.

ASSIGNMENT

1. Keep looking for opportunities to serve others at home, at work, and in the community.
2. Each family member do one act of service during the coming week. Then, at the next lesson, share what you did.
3. If you wish, as a family do one (or both) of the Additional Activities that follow: Taped Books and Form Letter.

ADDITIONAL ACTIVITY
TAPED BOOKS

In many families, reading aloud is an enjoyable tradition. Listening to familiar voices and reading favorite stories help children feel loved and secure. It also helps develop a life-long appreciation for books. Adults benefit too because it provides a chance for parents to bond with their children.

In today's families, members don't always live together in the same household. However, as the following activity shows, distance doesn't have to interfere with the closeness that comes from reading aloud. As parents, grandparents, aunts and uncles, etc., you can still read aloud to younger family members even though you live miles apart.

ACTIVITY INSTRUCTIONS

1. Buy or borrow one or two books suitable to the listener's age and interest level. If you need guidance in selecting the books, you might want to consult with guides such as the following:

    > Kimmel, Margaret Mary, and Elizabeth Segel. *For Reading Out Loud!: A Guide to Sharing Books with Children.* New York: Delacorte Press, 1988.

    > Trelease, Jim. *The Read-Aloud Handbook.* New York: Penguin Books, 2001.

2. Read the books before making thetape so you are familiar with the story and vocabulary.
3. Now, read the book aloud as you tape.

    • First, explain how glad you are to be reading to them.

    • Next, give the title and author of the book.

    •Read slowly and naturally, as though the listener were sitting beside you.

4. When the tape is filled, mail it (with the book, if you desire) in a padded envelope.

Note: Younger family members can read to elderly relatives also.

ADDITIONAL ACTIVITY

FORM LETTER

Dear _____,

Hello! How are you? We are trying to write more often, and our family thinks using this form letter will help us. You might be interested to know that _____ _____ _____.

It's been really _____because _____ _____.

The weather here has been

( ) rainy   ( ) sunny   ( ) gorgeous   ( ) windy
( ) snowy   ( ) gloomy   ( ) warm   ( ) heavenly
( ) foggy   ( ) hot   ( ) nasty   ( ) stormy
( ) muddy   ( ) humid   ( ) yucky   ( ) other

and so I have been _____ _____.Things have been pretty_____ at our house. _____is/are _____,and that means that _____. Last week,_____had to _____because _____. _____ says to tell you _____ _____.

He/She is_____and will probably_____before too much longer.

One wonderful/terrible/exciting/interesting thing that happened to me recently was ____ _____ _____.I felt really_____about it because _____ _____ _____.Before I go, I just want to say _____ _____ and I hope you_____ _____.

Fondly,

Lesson Eight
Traditions

If we will build righteous traditions in our families, the light of the gospel can grow even brighter in the lives of our children from generation to generation.

—Elder L. Tom Perry (*Ensign*, May 1990, 20)

FOLLOW-UP

(As a family, discuss the assignment for the lesson "Service.")

1. How are we doing in our efforts to be like the Sea of Galilee—giving of ourselves to others?
2. Has anyone done a service they'd like to tell us about?
3. How did we do with our family service project this month?

CONCEPT

A family tradition is an activity that a family does regularly. Often traditions are so simple that families don't even recognize them as traditions. For example, if a family always has special birthday celebrations, that's a tradition. If they like to eat certain kinds of food on Sundays, that's a tradition. Any activity repeated over and over becomes a tradition, and families share those happy memories. President Ezra T. Benson suggested, "As a family, go on

campouts and picnics, to ball games and recitals, to school programs . . . Build traditions of family vacations and trips and outings. These memories will never be forgotten" (*Ensign,* Nov. 1987, 51). The personalities of families are expressed through the little things they do that add fun to life.

Elder James E. Faust suggested, "Develop family traditions. Some of the great strengths of families can be found in their own traditions, which may consist of many things: making special occasions of the blessing of children, baptisms, ordinations to the priesthood, birthdays, fishing trips, skits on Christmas Eve, family home evening, and so forth. The traditions of each family are unique" (*Ensign,* May 1983, 41).

Healthy relationships are built on time spent together. Family traditions create opportunities for us to be with one another. As we join together and participate in a tradition, we share our lives in special ways that are unique to our family. Usually, the more we share our lives, the more we care for one another. Elder Donald L. Hallstrom remarked, "Uplifting traditions play a significant role in leading us toward the things of the Spirit. Those that promote love for Deity and unity in families and among people are especially important" (*Ensign,* Nov. 2000, 28).

A family is like a chain, and family members are like the links in the chain. Experiences shared together strengthen and bind these links. Traditions strengthen family links by giving family members a sense of belonging, something to depend on in a world that is constantly changing. Our time together as a family is priceless. The memories we make will last throughout our lifetimes.

FAMILY SURVEY REVIEW
Statement 8: We have family traditions.

- Why is it important for a family to have traditions?
- What are some of our family traditions?

STORY

One winter a mother took a group of high school students on a night-snowshoeing trip to a friend's cabin. The moon was beautiful and full as it shone on the new-fallen snow. For nearly five miles they puffed and plodded along. The first mile or two still held the excitement and mystery of an adventure. But as time wore on, tired legs could scarcely drag nearly frozen toes from drift to drift up the mountainside. The backpacks were no help either. And every few minutes someone's snowshoe straps would come loose or break, sending that person flying into a snowbank head first.

No one complained much, though, because they all knew a warm cabin was waiting at the top.

When the group finally reached the cabin and worked the old door open, they gasped as they looked around. Windows were broken, the kitchen table had three legs and a stump, three rusty springs showed through the upholstery on the couch, and the cabin itself seemed very small. Months before, someone had left the chimney flue open, and frozen snow was jammed in the fireplace all the way to the roof. One teenager picked away at the solid block with a pocketknife, while another went to the kitchen to start the wood-burning stove. Disaster again! The stovepipe had separated and was also packed with snow. It was frighteningly cold, and the cabin was quickly filling with the choking smoke. Everyone was complaining and feeling sorry for themselves.

"Hey!" the mother who led the group shouted. "There's a new rule. For every complaint you make, you've got to say something good as well." More grumbles. She added, "Well, what have we got to lose? We can at least die with positive attitudes!" Everyone chuckled softly.

"But I'm freezing," one young man complained. The woman smiled and waited patiently. "Uh," he choked, "but at least the smoke is warming the place up."

"Three of the four windows are broken," a girl grumbled. Then she brightened. "At least they draw out the smoke. Should we break the other one?" That brought a real laugh.

As the woman poked in the fire, billows of smoke seeped from every crack in the old stove. She hoped it would melt some of the ice above. After unloading each arm-load of wood, one pair of students rushed to open the door and draw a few fresh breaths of cold mountain air. Two others alternately fanned the fire and dashed for the door to breathe, while one boy struggled with the broken stovepipe.

Gradually the smoke began to clear. As the snow in the stovepipe melted, the cabin warmed up, and so did their spirits. Before long the campers had a big pot of hot soup on the stove, and the young people were sitting on their rolled-out sleeping bags, happily sipping hot drinks.

Without exception, the memories of that trip were good ones. No one seems to remember the grumbles or the complaints. The mother who led the group started a new tradition in her family. Whenever someone has a complaint, he or she always has to add something positive afterward. She believes this tradition will help her family through any challenge.[40]

DISCUSSION

1. How can this family's new tradition help them through their challenges?
2. If we said something positive after complaining, could it help us?
3. Has our family ever started a tradition without planning it?

ACTIVITY

Our activity for this lesson is to decide on a new tradition for our family. Some ideas are listed below. We can use one of these or think of our own.

- Declare a "Be-Kind-to-(name)-Week." Do something nice for the person every day that week.
- On birthdays, take turns telling the birthday person one reason why you love or appreciate him or her.
- Create a "Memory Wall" in your home, consisting of important events in the family, from school plays to family trips.
- Once a week play board games as a family and then enjoy treats.
- Have a cookie-decorating contest every Valentine's Day or St. Patrick's Day.
- Read the scriptural accounts of Christ's birth on Christmas Eve, and of His Crucifixion and Resurrection at Easter.
- Prepare a special dish that your family eats each week at the same time (like home-made waffles every Sunday).
- Give family members love notes in lunch sacks, on desks, on mirrors, etc.
- When you're traveling, try to find license plates from each of the fifty states.
- Give father's blessings to each child at the beginning of the school year.
- Give a rose to your mother on your birthday.
- Have the birthday person choose the menu and excuse him or her from chores.
- Go to the library once a week as a family.

ASSIGNMENT

1. Plan the details of a new family tradition. Everyone in your family can help with some part of this tradition.
2. Do the Additional Activity: Family Scavenger Hunt.
3. Read Additional Solution for Success: Family Hobby.

ADDITIONAL ACTIVITY
FAMILY SCAVENGER HUNT

Many things in our homes have a story behind them, or they're related to a tradition. This activity is intended to help families strengthen their feelings of family pride and history by learning about special family possessions.

ACTIVITY INSTRUCTIONS

1. Make a list of things you're going to hunt for. Use the Scavenger Hunt List below or make your own.

2. Have family members work individually or in teams. Set a time limit.

3. After the time has expired, gather everyone together to see what they've found. Have each person show the things they found.

4. Talk about each item and explain why it is special to your family.

Scavenger Hunt List:

- Find something in your house that used to belong to somebody else.
- Write the name of a food that everyone enjoys having for dinner.
- Count the total number of books you have in your house.
- Write the color of paint, bedspreads, or curtains that you used to have in your house before the current decor.
- Find an object that represents something everyone in your family likes to do together for fun.
- Find something that is older than the oldest person living there.
- Find something that is broken or that doesn't work anymore.
- Find something that represents one of your family's special traditions.
- Find something that was bought in another state or foreign country.
- Find a tape, CD, or movie everyone in your family likes.
- Find the oldest photograph you have.
- Find something that reminds you of one of the happiest moments that have occurred in your family.
- If you were moving away and could only take a small four-foot by five-foot trailer with you, what family possessions would you pack?
- If a flood was coming and you could only save one thing from your house (besides your family), what would you take?

ADDITIONAL SOLUTION FOR SUCCESS

FAMILY HOBBY

A hobby is an activity that is done for pleasure. One of the things that makes families work well is participating in a hobby together. This requires effort on the part of family members, but the more you share your lives, the more you'll enjoy one another.

Have each family member write on a paper what they would like to do for a family hobby. Collect the papers and read them, making only positive remarks about the ideas.

Suggestions for possible hobbies:

- Gardening

- Bicycling

- Camping

- Cooking

- Self-defense (taking lessons, competing, etc.)

- Music (playing musical instruments, attending concerts, etc.)

- Hiking

- Collecting things (stamps, antiques, etc.)

- Traveling

- Art (drawing, painting, etc.)

- Sewing

- Fishing

- Boating

- Woodwork

After all the ideas for a family hobby have been read, discuss what would be the best hobby for your family. You may decide on two or three hobbies!

Choose a family hobby and schedule a day to begin. Discuss what you'll need for your hobby and assign family members to get what is needed. Perhaps you'll want some instruction. If so, contact someone to teach your family about the hobby you've chosen. During your weekly family meeting, schedule dates regularly to participate in your hobby.

SOLUTIONS THROUGH STORIES AND POEMS: COMMITTMENT

DETERMINATION

Nowadays the four-minute mile is commonplace for champion runners, but at one time it was scarcely thought possible. The man who proved it could be done was the British medical student Roger Bannister—the man with the will to win.

He had been disappointed at his performance in the 1952 Olympic Games and had just about decided to give up on running and concentrate on his medical training. He told his coach this.

"Roger," said his coach, "I think you are the man who can break the four-minute mile. I wish you would give it one last chance before you quit."

Roger went home and thought about this. Before the night was over, he had crystallized in his mind, in the form of an iron will, the determination that he was going to break the four-minute-mile barrier before he quit running.

He knew what he must do. He would have to study between eight and ten hours a day in order to get through medical school and he would also have to train for four hours a day, run to build up his body to peak perfection, go to bed early, and sleep nine to ten hours a night so that his body could recuperate—all this to build up for that great day. He was willing to pay this price in addition to his previous training. For several months he went through a routine just like that.

Finally came the day for the four-minute mile. It was a bad day for the competition. It had rained for five hours and there was a sharp wind blowing, which made it a slow track. But Roger was not deterred. He told his running mates what he was going to try for. They encouraged him, shook his hand, and said they would do what they could to help by pacing him.

The first lap was right on time—57.5 seconds. Because of the slow track, all the runners had to push in order to maintain that pace for the second lap, but when they finished it they were still on time—1 minute 58.2 seconds. Then they went into the third lap, the hardest of all, when fatigue starts setting in. Roger and his running mates were tired, but at the end of the third lap they were still on time—3 minutes and 0.5 seconds in all. They were on their way to the first four-minute mile in history.

Roger said afterward that he had never been so tired in his life as when he started that fourth lap. As he went around that first turn, his steps began to falter and he felt dead. His head was throbbing, his lungs were bursting, and his mind began to say to him, "Slacken up, and just try for a win." But, as if in reply, something welled up inside of him and said, "Roger, if you run until you collapse on this track, you are going to make this four-minute mile. If your knees hit this track, you are going to do it. For all these months you have trained, and you've got to." So instead of slacking the pace, he fought off the pain, picked up his knees and began sprinting. Numb and tired as his legs were, he forced them to go.

As he hit the last curve, again his stride began to break. Describing it later, he said that there seemed to be an eternity in those fifty yards to the tape. But he closed his eyes, gritted his teeth, and forced himself to hold stride as he pounded down the stretch. Finally, he took that one last step which broke the tape, and he collapsed into the arms of his coach. His time was 3 minutes 59.4 seconds. Roger Bannister had broken through the four-minute-mile barrier.[41]

BOY, WE REALLY HAVE A SWELL BATHROOM, DON'T WE?

It was a gorgeous October day. My husband, Art, and I were down at the boat landing helping our friend Don drag his skiff up on the beach. Art remarked wistfully that it would be a long time before next summer when we could all start sailing again. "You folks ought to take up skiing like our family and have fun the year round," Don said.

"Doesn't that get pretty expensive?" I asked.

Don straightened up and smiled. "It's funny," he said. "We live in an old-fashioned house—legs on the tub, that sort of thing. For years we've been saving up to have the bathroom done over. But every winter we take the money out of the bank and go on a couple of family skiing trips. Our oldest boy is in the army now, and he often mentions in his letters what a great time we had on those trips. You know, I can't imagine his writing home, 'Boy, we really have a swell bathroom, don't we?'"[42]

EVERYONE CRIES, "THERE WASN'T TIME."

Time. It hangs heavy for the bored, eludes the busy, flies by for the young and runs out for the aged.

Time. We talk about it like it's a manufactured commodity that some can afford, others can't; some can reproduce, others waste. We crave it. We curse it. We kill it. We abuse it. Is it a friend? Or an enemy? I suspect we know very little about it. To know it all and its potential, perhaps we should view it through a child's eyes.

"When I was young, Daddy was going to throw me up in the air and catch me and I would giggle until I couldn't giggle anymore, but he had to change the furnace filter and there wasn't time."

"When I was young, Mama was going to read me a story and I was going to turn the pages and pretend I could read, but she had to wax the bathroom and there wasn't time."

"When I was young, Daddy was going to come to school and watch me in a play. I was the fourth Wise Man (in case one of the three got sick), but he had an appointment to have his car tuned up and it took longer than he thought and there was no time."

"When I was young, Mama was going to listen to me read my essay on 'What I Want to Be When I Grow Up,' but she was in the middle of the Monday Night Movie and Gregory Peck was always one of her favorites and there wasn't time."

"When I was older, Dad and I were going fishing one weekend, just the two of us, and we were going to pitch a tent and fry fish with the heads on them like they do in the flashlight ads, but at the last minute he had to fertilize the grass and there wasn't time."

"When I was older, the whole family was always going to pose together for our Christmas card, but my brother had ball practice, my sister had her hair up, Dad was watching the Colts, and Mom had to wax the bathroom. There wasn't time."

"When I grew up and left home to be married, I was going to sit down with Mom and Dad and tell them I loved [them] and I would miss them. But Hank (he was my best man and a real clown) was honking the horn in front of the house, so there wasn't time."

—Contributed by Erma Bombeck[43]

MY FRIEND

I love you, not only for what you are, but for what I am when I am with you. I love you, not only for what you have made of yourself, but for what you are making of me. I love you for the part of me that you bring out; I love you for putting your hand into my heaped-up heart and passing over all the foolish, weak things that you can't help dimly seeing there and for drawing out into the light all of the beautiful belongings that no one else had looked quite far enough to find.

I love you because you are helping me to make of the lumber in my life not a tavern, but a temple; out of the works every day not a reproach, but a song.

I love you because you have done more than any creed could have done to make me good, and more than any fate could have done to make me happy. You have done it without touch, without a word, without a sign. You have done it by being yourself. Perhaps that is what being a friend means, after all.

—Contributed by Ray Croft[44]

TWELVE GUIDEPOSTS FOR LIVING

I will do more than belong—I will participate.
I will do more than care—I will help.
I will do more than believe—I will practice.
I will do more than be fair—I will be kind.
I will do more than forgive—I will forget.
I will do more than dream—I will work.
I will do more than teach—I will inspire.
I will do more than earn—I will enrich.
I will do more than give—I will serve.
I will do more than live—I will grow.
I will do more than be friendly—I will be a friend.
I will do more than be a citizen—I will be a patriot.

—Author Unknown[45]

BE THE BEST OF WHATEVER YOU ARE

If you can't be a pine on the top of the hill,
Be a scrub in the valley—but be
The best little scrub by the side of the rill;
Be a bush if you can't be a tree.

If you can't be a bush be a bit of the grass,
And some highway happier make;
If you can't be a muskie then just be a bass—
But be the liveliest bass in the lake!

We can't all be captains, we've got to be crew.
There's something for all of us here,
There's big work to do, and there's lesser to do,
And the task you must do is near.

If you can't be a highway then just be a trail,
If you can't be the sun be a star;
It isn't by size that you win or you fail—
Be the best of whatever you are!
—Contributed by Douglas Malloch[46]

WHICH LOVED BEST?

"I love you, Mother," said little John;
Then, forgetting the work, his cap went on,
And he was off to the garden swing,
And left her the water and wood to bring.

"I love you, Mother," said rosy Nell—
"I love you better than tongue can tell;"
Then she teased and pouted full half the day,
Till her Mother rejoiced when she went to play.

"I love you, Mother," said little Fran.
"Today I'll help you all I can;
How glad I am that school doesn't keep!"
So she rocked the babe till it fell asleep.

Then stepping softly, she fetched the broom,
And swept the floor and tidied the room;
Busy and happy all day was she,
Helpful and happy as child can be.

"I love you, Mother," again they said,
Three little children going to bed;
How do you think that Mother guessed
Which of them really loved her best?
—Contributed by Joy Allison[47]

Chapter Three
Communication
Solution

Let no corrupt communication proceed out of your mouth, but that which is good.

—Ephesians 4:29

Introduction for Parents

I would like to begin by sharing two stories. The first is about communication between a husband and wife.

Robert was a new employee with his company. Getting established as a successful salesman demanded a great deal of time and energy, both physical and emotional.

> I would sometimes wake up at night in a cold sweat, feeling anxious about whether I would make it as a salesman. I worried about having enough money to make ends meet. Some months I made adequate income and some months I did not.
>
> I was becoming an emotional wreck, but didn't share my feelings with my wife, Sherie. I guess because I didn't think it was the macho thing to do. I wanted to appear strong and in control to her. But she wasn't fooled. One evening while we were walking in the park, she said, "Robert, you're feeling pretty uptight about how things are going at work, aren't you?" I told her that I was not tense at all, that everything was okay. She didn't let me off the hook. "Yes, you are worried," she insisted, "and I think it's natural. But I don't like to see you feel this way. Let's talk about it and see if your situation is as bad as it seems, and what we can do to make things better."
>
> At that point I opened up to her and shared all of my frustration and concerns. I felt like a dam had been opened up inside me. I had not talked with anyone about this, and it was a great relief to finally get it out. We talked about ways to cut our expenses and things we could live without.
>
> Then Sherie asked me, "What is the worst thing that could possibly happen?" I answered, "The worst thing is that I would lose my job." Then she reminded me that if I lost my job we would still be able to make it on her income, and her job was very stable. We would have to make some changes, but we could make it.
>
> That talk helped a great deal. My sales gradually increased, and today I'm one of the top salesmen for the company. But that's not the most important part of the story. The most important part is that on that evening years ago, Sherie was sensitive enough and interested in me enough to know that I was hurting and needed to talk. She cared enough to start the conversation. As a result of talking through that situation, I felt closer to Sherie than I ever had. I think that established our close bond with each other more than any other single event, and it set the pattern for that type of caring, open communication.[48]

This second story has been fictionalized for this book, but relates a truth about how the Spirit affecrs our ability to communicate.

One morning Suzanne received a phone call from the schoolteacher of her son Josh. Josh had been disrespectful to several teachers. Suzanne's temper flared, and she began to think of all the things she was going to tell Josh when he returned home that afternoon.

To make matters worse, Josh was late coming home from school because he was fighting with a neighbor boy. The fight continued all the way to her front lawn. At that point she stepped to the door and called to Josh, asking him to come in. He ignored her. Then Suzanne ordered her son to come in. Suzanne knew she was too angry to deal with the problem in the emotional state she was in, so she sent Josh to his room.

Shaking with anger, Suzanne slipped into her bedroom to kneel and pray. She prayed for wisdom in handling the problem, and also asked that through the Spirit she would know what to say. As she stood up after praying, she felt a warm, calm feeling consume her.

As she opened his door, Suzanne saw Josh sitting on his bed. She was filled with an understanding of, and a compassion for, the challenges and difficulties of a little boy in his situation.

She sat on the edge of the bed next to him and put her arm around his small shoulders. The first words she spoke surprised her, for she said, "Josh, forgive me for being cross with you." Then she told him of the phone call from his teacher and gave him an opportunity to explain himself. They had a wonderful talk; he confided in her, and, as they spoke, they did so in whispers. This was much different from the tone she had expected to use before asking Heavenly Father for help. She realized that it was a truly spiritual experience, and believed it did more for the relationship between Josh and herself than anything she could have imagined.

Communication is the process or way we transfer information from one person to another so that it is received and understood. *Received* and *understood* are the key words. We can't call it communication if one person talks and another only appears to listen. It is only communication—real communication—if information is received and understood.

Elder Marvin J. Ashton taught, "Often parents communicate most effectively with their children by the way they listen to and address each other. Their conversations showing gentleness and love are heard by our ever-alert, impressionable children. We must learn to communicate effectively not only by voice, but by tone, feelings, glances, mannerisms, and total personality" (*Ensign,* May 1976, 53).

We could say that communication is a two-way street with lots of traffic signs and billboards. To really communicate we have to be "reading the signs" as we drive and "watching for oncoming traffic." Let's look at those two sentences from three angles. First, "Communication is a two-way street." Two or more people need to be involved for communication to exist. If we, as parents, are the only ones talking, and our children are not listening, we are not communicating. There is a saying, "I don't care how much you know until I know how much you care." We need to be sure our children know without a doubt that we love them and that we truly care about their well-being. Then, with confidence in our love and concern for them, usually our children will more readily listen to us.

Elder Russell M. Nelson reminds us,

> The time to listen is when someone needs to be heard. Children are naturally eager
> to share their experiences, which range from triumphs of delight to trials of distress.
> Are we as eager to listen? If they try to express their anguish, is it possible for us to

listen openly to a shocking experience without going into a state of shock ourselves? Can we listen without interrupting and without making snap judgments that slam shut the door of dialogue? It can remain open with the soothing reassurance that we believe in them and understand their feelings (*Ensign,* May 1991, 22).

Second, I believe that as we communicate with our children, they give us "traffic signs and billboards" to both direct us and distract us. What our children say does not always reflect their honest, heartfelt feelings. As parents we need to be constantly "reading the signs" of our children's body language, facial expressions, and tones of voice. Sometimes we need to listen "between the lines" for what they are really saying and try to understand how they are honestly feeling. Peter Drucker once said, "The most important thing in communication is to hear what isn't being said."[49]

Four Parts of Good Communication

1. *Listening.* Listening strengthens relationships by showing that the listener cares about the person speaking. True listening involves hearing with the heart as well as with the ears.
2. *Rephrasing.* Rephrasing is restating the basic message in fewer or different words, to be sure you understand the speaker and to let them know you're listening and trying to understand.
3. *Probing.* The speaker is encouraged to say more when the listener asks questions. Probing directs the speaker's attention inward to examine his or her feelings and thoughts in more depth. This also shows caring and concern on the part of the listener.
4. *Positive Speaking.* Positive speaking shows kindness and demonstrates that relationships are valued.

Third, "watching for oncoming traffic" means that as we talk with our children we should expect occasional negative or hurtful words (oncoming traffic) that they don't really mean or that they unintentionally communicate badly. Again, we have choices. Three wrong ways we could react to unkind words are to be offended, to retaliate, or to stop talking. As parents we have the responsibility to teach our children productive behavior by our example. What we should say will vary by situation, so it is important to know a variety of good communication skills (like the ones listed above) and then to be sensitive and creative in our methods.

A key to communicating well with our children is to try to remember what it was like to be a child or young adult. Whether the one to whom you are speaking (or listening) is three, thirteen, or twenty-three, try while you are communicating to be that age in your mind, with their life experiences, needs, and desires. Then you will be able to use the understanding from that position and add it to the wisdom of your adulthood, the result being a wonderful place from which you can communicate with both empathy and discernment.

If we can put into practice what we've learned about speaking with kindness and combine it with sharing our hearts openly and listening with the intent to understand and help, we are on the road to communicating deeply and effectively. Strong relationships are built not on "surface talk," during which people only discuss the weather or other nonthreatening subjects. Usually relationships that stand the test of trials and time are those whose participants are willing to communicate the thoughts and honest feelings of their hearts. By doing so, people risk ridicule and rejection. Nonetheless, these people accept that risk because they cannot be satisfied with anything less than sincere, meaningful relationships.

Learning and strengthening communication skills doesn't mean that strong families don't have conflict. They do. Family members get angry with each other, misunderstand one another, and sometimes just disagree. But when they communicate, they're able to get their differences out in the open where they can discuss the problem and come to a satisfactory solution for everyone. That doesn't mean the solution will give all involved exactly what they want; it just means they've reached a common ground on which they can agree.

What are some of the advantages of positive, open communication? Family members who have learned to communicate well with one another have learned to talk and to listen carefully. They know and feel each other's joys and sorrows. They know how to laugh together. They enjoy a sense of humor that brings happiness to their lives. Families who communicate well are able to express openly their feelings, differences, similarities, and hopes for the future. They practice positive ways of handling conflict so problems are discussed openly, and solutions are found.

Good communication also provides security and safety. People know where they stand in the family, and that contributes to a feeling of well-being.

Sometimes we take family communication for granted. We may think we communicate well just because we're a family or because we spend a good deal of time together. However, we can all improve our communication skills.

Relationships are built one interaction at a time. Each interaction moves the relationship in a positive or negative way. We usually can't change relationships overnight, but making gradual improvements in our communication skills will make a big difference in the long run.

Lesson Nine
Understand First

If we could know true love and understanding one for another, we must realize . . . it is the wise sharing of emotions, feelings, and concerns. It is the sharing of oneself totally.

—Marvin J. Ashton (*Ensign*, May 1976, 52)

FOLLOW-UP

(As a family, discuss the assignment for the lesson "Traditions.")

1. What new tradition did our family start?
2. Do we all enjoy the new tradition? If not, let's talk about how we can make it better.

CONCEPT

Good communication is understanding and being understood. In our family we should be able to talk to one another easily. We should know that we can share our feelings in confidence, know that we won't be laughed at, and feel understood.

Trying to first understand before being understood means that we are more interested in others than in ourselves. It means that we really want to communicate, not just tell how we feel.

We can try to understand in three ways. First, we think about how the other person is feeling, with their life experiences and needs. We try to "be" that person for a moment. Second, we watch their body language (facial expression, posture) for clues that tell us how they're really feeling. Third, we listen very carefully, concentrating on what is being said, not on what we're going to say next.

When we make a real effort to understand before we try to be understood, usually our efforts will be appreciated, our communication will improve, and our relationships will become stronger and more loving.

To make communication work, we have to understand what people are trying to tell us. Here is a story of a man whom nobody understood:

A construction worker approached the reception desk in a doctor's office. The receptionist asked him why he was there. "I have shingles," he said. She took down his name, address, medical insurance number, and told him to have a seat.

Fifteen minutes later a nurse came out and asked him what he had. "Shingles," he replied. She took down his height, weight, and a complete medical history and told him to wait in the examining room.

A half hour later, a nurse came in and asked him why he was here. "I have shingles," he replied again. She took his blood pressure . . . and told him to take off his clothes and wait for the doctor.

An hour later, the doctor came in and asked him what he had. He said, "Shingles."

The doctor said, "Where?"

He said, "Outside in the truck. Where do you want them?"[50]

FAMILY SURVEY REVIEW
Statement 9: We try to understand one another's feelings.

- Why is it important to understand one another's feelings?
- When people really try to understand you, how does it make you feel?

STORY

Relate this fictionalized story to open a family discussion:

Early one Saturday morning a young father and his little son shared a lesson on understanding.

Danny was delighted when he found a black marking pen in the kitchen drawer. What fun he had drawing all over the new kitchen chairs! The fun was gone, however, when Dad walked in the room. "Danny! What have you done?" he asked in a loud voice. The little boy was scared. Danny's father scolded him angrily and took him to his room.

A few hours later, Danny's father found him in the middle of another mess. This time he had dumped a box of powdered soap all over a chair and the floor! The father grabbed Danny, ran all the way back to the boy's bedroom, spanked him, and left him there.

Returning to the kitchen, his father suddenly realized that Danny hadn't been making another mess. He had simply been trying to clean the ink off the chairs.

Feeling remorseful, his father recalled how Danny had looked at him right before he spanked him. The little boy's eyes had been filled with fear and hope for understanding. Realizing what he had done, the father went to his small son's room and humbly asked for forgiveness, then patiently taught Danny how to use markers correctly.

Later, the father realized that Danny wasn't the only one who had learned something that day. Dad had learned a valuable lesson about the importance of understanding people *first* before you try to be understood.

DISCUSSION

1. Right before his father spanked him, what did Danny want?
2. Name one way we can try to understand one another.

ACTIVITY

This activity teaches how to help people understand us when we communicate. We use "I messages." This is how it works:

"I Messages"	"Example"
1. Start with the word I.	"I . . .
2. Add what you're thinking, needing, etc.	need some help getting these dishes done . . .
3. Explain why.	. . . because I have to leave for work."

Now let's all take a turn. Let's each think of one "I message" to share with the family. See the following examples:

- "I feel upset when you're late because we all agreed to be home for dinner at six-thirty each night."
- "I appreciate it when you're on time. It shows me that you care about our rules."
- "I feel angry when you disobey because you know better."
- "I feel sad when you disobey because you helped make the family rules."
- "It makes me happy to see you share because I know you're doing the right thing."

ASSIGNMENT

The first part of the assignment is to make a real effort to understand people (especially family members) before you try to be understood. Now lets practice these new communication skills. It's not always *what* is said, but *how* it's said, that creates happiness or unhappiness.

"SAY"	"DON'T SAY"
• "I've noticed that sometimes you . . ."	• "You always . . ." or "You never . . ."
• "I feel upset when you . . ."	• "You make me angry when . . ."
• "Help me understand what you're thinking . . ."	• "Why do you . . ."
• "You seem upset . . ."	• "You are angry, so . . ."
• "I'm feeling annoyed when you . . ."	• "I hate it when you . . ."
• "I appreciate it when you do . . . but it bothers me when you . . ."	• "It bothers me when you..."
• "I understand that you're feeling . . . can I share my thoughts with you?"	• "Listen to me!"

You may also participate in the Additional Activity or read the Additional Solution for Success: Who's Who in the Family, or Communication Skills to Strengthen Family Relationships.

ADDITIONAL ACTIVITY

WHO'S WHO IN THE FAMILY

Name_____ Age _____ Sex _____
Position in the Family: _____
What do you like about being in this position?_____
_____
_____

What don't you like about being in this position? _____
_____
_____
_____

What do you like best about yourself? _____
_____
_____
_____

What would you like to change about yourself?_____
_____
_____
_____

What things do you like best about your family?_____
_____
_____
_____

What things do you wish were different about your family? _____
_____
_____
_____

Thoughts I would like to share with my family: _____
_____
_____
_____

ADDITIONAL SOLUTION FOR SUCCESS

COMMUNICATION SKILLS TO STRENGTHEN FAMILY RELATIONSHIPS

- **Communicate and listen.** Focus on attentive listening and "hear" the feelings behind the words. Parents, listen to your children talk about how things are today. Try to see through their eyes and help them see through yours.

- **Affirm and support one another.** Parents, recognize that your role is to guide and influence and that your child may decide to live differently than you. Allow for differences without withdrawing your love and acceptance.

- **Respect each other.** Show respect for one another's ideas and each person's contributions to the family.

- **Develop trust.** Build a base of friendship and trust with one another. Minimize nagging and yelling; maximize friendly discussion.

- **Have a sense of play and humor.** Set aside time for fun with your family, such as taking walks, listening to music, playing games together, etc.

- **Share the responsibilities.** Build important skills by having all family members participate in decision making whenever possible.

- **Teach a sense of right and wrong.** Parents, teach your children by setting good examples for them. Make sure your children play a part in making the family rules and deciding on consequences. One way we gain a sense of right and wrong is by experiencing the consequences of a broken rule.

- **Nurture rituals and traditions.** Find ways family members can feel important and part of the family structure: sharing chores, cooking, helping pay the bills, planning a trip, or simply telling one another what makes them special in your family.

- **Foster family table time and talks.** Begin family meetings where everyone can share their ideas and be heard. Eat dinner without the TV.

- **Admit to and seek help for problems.** Don't hesitate to get help. Families are finding help and alternatives in support groups and local agencies throughout the country.

Lesson Ten
Positive Words

Members of the Church, young or old, should never allow pro-
fane or vulgar words to pass their lips. The language we use proj-
ects the images of our hearts, and our hearts should be pure.
—Elder Dallin H. Oaks (*Ensign*, May 1986, 51)

FOLLOW-UP

(As a family, discuss the assignment for the lesson "Understand First.")

1. How are we doing in our efforts to try to understand before we try to be understood?
2. Has someone made progress in this area that they would like to share with the family?

CONCEPT

Communication can be negative (unkind) or positive (kind). When we speak unkindly to one another, we destroy the loving atmosphere we want in our homes, and it makes family members feel unhappy and unloved. On the other hand, when we speak in a positive and kind way to one another, our family is happier. Those who hear praise, encouragement, and loving words usually have good feelings about themselves, and they can more easily be loving and thoughtful to others.

Let's show our appreciation and love to each other by the way we talk. Elder L. Lionel Kendrick reminds us, "We will be held accountable for all that we say. The Savior has warned 'that every idle word that men shall speak, they shall give account thereof in the day of judgment' (Matt. 12:36). This means that no communication shall be without consequence. This includes the slight slips of the tongue, the caustic communications that canker the soul, and the vain, vulgar, and profane words which desecrate the name of Deity" (*Ensign*, Nov. 1988, 23).

How we're spoken to often determines how we feel about ourselves. Those feelings, either good or bad, help determine our self-talk. An example of negative self-talk is, "I'm so stupid!" An example of good self-talk is to think, "That's not like me. I usually don't make mistakes like that."

Self-fulfilling prophecies are things people say to us that sometimes affect the way we act. For example, if a child is told, "You'll never be a good athlete!" he may believe it and never improve his athletic skills. On the other hand, positive comments work wonders. For example, when parents say to their daughter, "You are a very obedient girl!" they encourage obedience by helping the child believe she always obeys. It is so important to speak positively because people usually become what they are told they are.

Below are some negative and positive comments that can help determine behavior and character:

Negative	Positive
• "You'll probably fight over this new toy."	• "I know you're going to share this new toy because you are sharing children."
• "You are so disobedient!"	• "I'm sure you'll obey right away next time because you usually obey so quickly."
• "It's about time!"	• "Thanks so much."
• "Well, somebody finally gave in!"	• "You're such a peacemaker in our family. Doesn't that make you feel good when you choose the right?"
• "You kids are always quarreling!"	• "It's not like you to quarrel. You usually get along so well."
• "Mom, you never understand me!"	•"Mom, usually you try to understand me. Could you try a little harder to see how I feel about this?"

FAMILY SURVEY REVIEW
Statement 10: We speak kindly to one another and try not to criticize.

- How does our family generally speak to one another?
- How can we be more positive and less critical of each other?

STORY

In a small town in Spain, a man named Jorge had a bitter argument with his young son Paco. The next day Jorge discovered that Paco's bed was empty—he had run away from home.

Overcome with remorse, Jorge searched his soul and realized that his son was more important to him than anything else. He wanted to start over. Jorge went to a well-known store in the center of town and posted a large sign that read, "Paco, come home. I love you. Meet me here tomorrow morning."

The next morning Jorge went to the store where he found no less than seven young boys named Paco who had also run away from home. They were all answering the call for love, each one hoping it was his dad inviting him home with open arms.

—Contributed by Alan Cohen[51]

DISCUSSION

    1. Sometimes do we say things in anger that we don't really mean?
    2. We all want to be loved. Name some ways we can communicate love to others.

ACTIVITY

For our activity we're going to change negative statements into positive ones. Let's take turns and do one statement at a time.

Negative	Positive
• "You are a slow runner!"	• "With practice you can be a fast runner!"
• "I can't do that."	• "I can do that."
• "You never agree with me!"	• "Usually we agree on things. Can you try looking at it this way?"
• "How can you be so stupid?"	• "You know, I've made that same mistake myself!"
• "I hate you!"	• "I feel really angry at what you did!"
• "I'm ugly."	• "I want to look better."
• "Our family can't spell."	• "Spelling isn't what we're best at, but look at all the words you spelled right!"
• "You can't ever do anything right!"	• "You usually do this well. Why don't you try it this way . . ."
• "Our family never has any fun!"	• "I'd like to have more fun with our family. How about if we . . ."
• "Shut up!"	• "Please be quiet."

ASSIGNMENT

Choose one or more of the following assignments:

    1. Try each day to turn negative comments into positive ones. Remember that any habit is hard to break. Be kind to yourselves and have patience with one another as you try to improve. As you help one another speak more positively, it will be easito improve.
    2. Do the Additional Activity: Family Storybook.
    3. Read the Additional Solution for Success: Positive Speaking.

ADDITIONAL ACTIVITY
FAMILY STORYBOOK

Most people think there's something special about their family, and that feeling strengthens family unity. Family members share good times and bad, ordinary days and special occasions. Every family has a rich store of experiences, traditions, and memories that are meaningful to them. This activity can help you think about some of the things that make your family special.

Activity Instructions

- Explain that everyone who wants to participate can help write and illustrate a special book about the family. Discuss some things family members might write about from the list below, or make up your own ideas.
- Encourage family members to write as many "stories" as they want. It is a good idea to have them plan what they want to write about and even to try a rough draft before copying the final version into the book.

- Decide on a "deadline" for having all stories ready to put in the book.

- Encourage family members who enjoy drawing and coloring to illustrate their stories.

- Include snapshots and photographs where appropriate.

- Set up a time when everyone can be involved in putting the book together.

- Once the book has been written, don't stop there. Keep it up to date by encouraging family members to add more writing and art from time to time.

Storybook Suggestions

Depending on the ages of the children, suggest that family members consider the following options for telling your family's story:

Preschool and Young Elementary School Children:

- Draw pictures that illustrate what other family members have written.
- Suggest an event that young children will be able to remember and tell about (for example, the funniest thing Mom ever did, the time Dad fell off the sofa, why we love our pet, etc. Have the child dictate his or her description of the event to a parent or older brother or sister. Be sure to copy word for word what is said).

Older Elementary School Children:

- Describe a family tradition, outing, or other event that holds special meaning for you.
- Describe a funny incident or "inside joke" that involves your family.
- Write about your family from the point of view of the family's pet dog or cat.
- Write about yourself—your special hobbies, your favorite things to do, your likes and dislikes, etc.
- Describe something about your family that's different from other families.
- Write about what it's like to be_____years old.

Teenagers and Young Adults:

- Describe various aspects of family life (for example, a typical Monday morning, what happens at dinner time, how family chores are divided, etc.).
- Describe the family as if you were writing a special feature about them for a newspaper or magazine.
- Write about why the family's pet is just like another member of the family.
- Describe one of the happiest/saddest/funniest/scariest/most exciting things that ever happened to the family.
- Write about what it means to be a big brother or sister.
- Describe your earliest memories of younger brothers and sisters.

Parents:

- Write a family history or time line that includes important dates and milestones in the family's life.
- Describe the different places the family has lived.
- Keep a section for jotting down all those interesting things children say.
- Describe what it means to be a parent.
- Write about family members who are no longer living but will always be remembered in loving ways.

ADDITIONAL SOLUTION FOR SUCCESS
POSITIVE SPEAKING

Positive speaking shows kindness. It aims at strengthening relationships by building up the other person.

What are the benefits of positive speaking?

1. You have the opportunity to express yourself. If you speak in a positive way, people will listen to you more readily. That gives you opportunities to influence people for good.

2. It helps build a positive self-image. Speaking positively by giving praise, compliments, and words of appreciation is a wonderful way to build a person's self-image.

3. It builds trust in a relationship. Sincere, positive speaking tells people you are not trying to manipulate or take advantage of them; it encourages them to trust you.

4. It encourages cooperation. Positive speaking encourages cooperation and friendship.

5. It promotes honest, open communication. A person will usually open up and speak honestly and frankly with someone who has shown they care by speaking kindly.

Focusing on the positive while speaking to others helps put life and relationships in perspective, especially when things seem to be going badly. It says, "We are in this together, and we are going to win."

Marital therapist Richard Stuart believes that uncensored communication may be more than a relationship can bear. We shouldn't say hurtful, unkind things simply because we believe them to be true. Strong families understand this and work toward a type of measured honesty that is kind. Too often people use the excuse "I'm only being honest" to be overly critical. This is destructive to relationships. Be sensitively honest, speak positively, and always be kind.[52]

Lesson Eleven

Listening

Listening is more than being quiet. Listening is much more than silence. Listening requires undivided attention. The time to listen is when someone needs to be heard. The time to deal with a person with a problem is when he has the problem. The time to listen is the time when our interest and love are vital to the one who seeks our ear, our heart, our help, and our empathy.

—Elder Marvin J. Ashton (*Ensign*, May 1976, 53)

FOLLOW-UP

(As a family, discuss the assignment for the lesson "Positive Words.")

1. How are we improving with using positive words instead of negative ones?
2. Can anyone share an experience they've had with positive or negative self-talk?

CONCEPT

Listening is more than just hearing words. It is trying to understand a person's message and their feelings. When we listen, it shows that we care. Careful listening also increases our empathy for people's feelings. Empathy means to put yourself mentally in the other person's place so you can better understand their thoughts and concerns. Listening with empathy is one of the greatest gifts we can give another person.

When we listen we should:

1. Show we're listening. We can do this by facing the person, maintaining eye contact, and having an interested facial expression.
2. Be interested in what the person is saying and concentrate on their words.
3. Never interrupt.

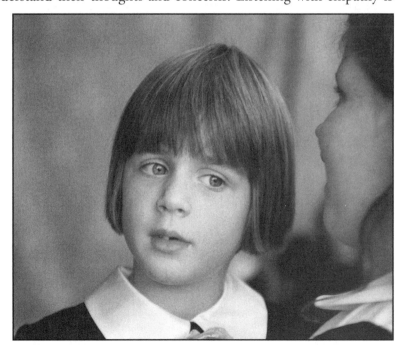

4. Watch the speaker's body language. We all communicate much through our facial expressions, posture, etc.

5. Actively listen. We should check if we understand by paraphrasing or repeating what the speaker says occasionally. This lets them know we're listening and interested.

6. Respond kindly. When the time is right, we should use empathy as we share our feelings about what has been said in a way that will help the person.

Elder Marvin J. Ashton remarked, "We should all increase our ability to ask comfortable questions, and then listen—intently, naturally. Listening is a tied-in part of loving" (*Ensign*, May 1976, 53).

Listening with love is a virtue we should all desire and seek to acquire. As we listen with open hearts and minds to the messages we hear, we will learn much and discover how we can best contribute to the happiness of others.

President Spencer W. Kimball told us, "Jesus was a listening leader. Because he loved others with a perfect love, he listened without being condescending. A great leader listens not only to others, but also to his conscience and to the promptings of God" (*Ensign*, Aug. 1974, 5).

FAMILY SURVEY REVIEW
Statement 11: We listen to each other.

- Are we good listeners in our family?
- How could we be better?

STORY

This is a story that tells how Thomas Edison, a famous American inventor, made a lot of money simply by using his ears instead of his mouth:

When the Western Union Company offered to buy Thomas Edison's newly invented telegraph ticker, Edison had no idea how much to ask for it. He asked for, and was granted, a few days to think about the purchase price.

Edison and his wife talked about the offer. Although stunned by Mrs. Edison's suggestion to ask for $20,000, he hesitantly agreed and set out to meet Western Union officials.

"What price have you decided on?" the Western Union representative asked.

When Edison attempted to tell him $20,000, the figure stuck to the roof of his mouth. He stood speechless for a moment. Impatient with the silence, the Western Union businessperson finally blurted, "How about $100,000 for the invention?"[53]

DISCUSSION

1. Did it help Thomas Edison to be silent for a moment instead of speaking when the Western Union buyer wanted to make a deal?
2. Why is it a good idea sometimes to listen instead of jumping in to speak?
3. How do we feel when people listen to us?

Activity

For this activity we need one person to be the speaker and one person to be the listener. First, the speaker will tell the listener something interesting that happened to them anytime in their life. The listener should use the six listening skills from the lesson:

1. Show you're listening. (Face the person, have eye contact, show interest.)
2. Be interested and concentrate.
3. Don't interrupt.
4. Watch the speaker's body language.
5. Actively listen. (Paraphrase or repeat what the speaker says.)
6. Respond kindly.

Second, after the speaker finishes, the two participants switch roles and the listener becomes the speaker.

Assignment

Choose one or more of the following assignments:
1. Be more aware of how you listen to others. Help one another improve your listening skills. Here's an example: If you're speaking to a family member who isn't looking at you, say something like, "I sometimes forget too, but do you remember that we're trying to look at each other when we talk and listen?"

2. Do the Additional Activity on the following page: Family Oral History.

3. Read the Additional Solution for Success: Listening.

ADDITIONAL ACTIVITY
FAMILY ORAL HISTORY

Grandparents, great-grandparents, and older relatives love to talk about their memories. Listening to them helps us understand what their lives were like. It allows us to learn first-hand from their experiences and to discover why your heritage is so special. In the following activity you'll make a tape recording of older family members to capture the past that may become a cherished family possession.

ACTIVITY INSTRUCTIONS

1. Arrange in advance to interview someone in your family.
2. Schedule a time and a quiet place for the interview. Be sure to choose a place where you won't be disturbed by other people or by background noises that would affect the quality of the tape.
3. Make a list of questions you want to ask. Try to create questions that prompt a story, not ones that can be answered with a simple yes or no.

SAMPLE QUESTIONS

A. About You:
- Where were you born?
- What were you like when you were my age?
- What did you do for fun?
- What kind of pets did you have?
- What was it like going to school?
- Where did you live? What was your house like?
- Did you have brothers and sisters? Did you get along?
- When did you meet Grandma/Grandpa?
- Do you remember your first date ever? What was he/she like?
- What were your parents like? What did they do for a living?
- How did you celebrate holidays? What foods did you eat?
- Did your family have any traditions? What were they?

B. About the Times You Grew Up In:
- Were you ever in a war? Tell me about it.
- What radio programs did you listen to?
- Do you remember when you bought your first television set?
- Did you watch the first astronauts land on the moon?

C. About Me:
- When was the first time you ever saw me?
- What was I like when I was a baby?
- Am I like my mom/dad when she/he was young?
- What do you think life will be like when I'm your age?

ADDITIONAL SOLUTION FOR SUCCESS

LISTENING

In the manual "Celebrating Family Strengths," researchers at the University of Oklahoma's Southwest Prevention Center offer valuable information about the skill of listening. They write, "Don't think all listening is something you do just for others. There are some great payoffs for those who listen."

Benefits for listeners:

1. *You gain knowledge.* You can learn a great deal of new information about people and ideas when you listen. This increases understanding of what is meant, as well as of what is said.

2. *Listening stimulates the speaker's expression of ideas and feelings.* When you know you are being listened to sincerely and with empathy, you're encouraged to continue speaking and to express your heartfelt ideas and feelings.

3. *You become a trusted person.* How many times have we heard the statement "to have a friend you must be one"?
This applies to families, too. When you listen well you are building trust with the speaker, who feels relaxed, comfortable, and secure in your attention.

4. *Good listening encourages cooperation from others.* When you are genuine in your attention, you encourage others to be genuine as well. Sincere interest in your family members often leads to respect and cooperation. This, in turn, can foster a sharing of ideas and a sense of mutual accomplishment.

5. *You can reduce tension and prevent trouble.* That can benefit both you and the speaker. Your careful listening gives the other person a chance to "let off steam" before he or she reaches the boiling point. If you learn to listen carefully before you speak, you often can prevent many minor problems before they become major ones.

6. *Listening can be fun.* Active listening, or listening with your heart as well as your ears, can increase your enjoyment in everything you do. You may actually learn to hear on higher, more positive levels of communication.

For many people, learning to listen is difficult. Many societies emphasize speaking, and the other end of the communication is often ignored. Communication is not a one-way street; it requires both speaking and listening.[54]

Lesson Twelve
Open Communication

Nothing is more important to the relationship between family members than open, honest communication.
—Elder M. Russell Ballard (*Ensign*, May 1999, 86–87)

FOLLOW-UP

(As a family, discuss the assignment for the lesson "Listening.")

1. What have we been doing to listen more carefully?
2. Can someone share an experience of a family member listening to him or her?

CONCEPT

One characteristic of a strong family is communication that is kind, open, frequent, and honest. Sometimes we expect others to know exactly what we want, or need, even when we say little or nothing at all. Elder Marvin J. Ashton said, "How important it is to be willing to voice one's thoughts and feelings. Yes, how important it is to be able to converse on the level of each family member. Too often we are inclined to let family members assume how we feel toward them. Often wrong conclusions are reached. Very often we could have performed better had we known how family members felt about us and what they expected" (*Ensign*, May 1976, 53).

Perhaps unkind remarks by others keep us from being open and honest—we're afraid of being hurt or embarrassed. It's very important that family members say only kind, supportive things when someone is sharing their feelings. We should never laugh or criticize in any way. Instead, we should try to understand how the person is feeling and listen with the intent to help.

When we can say what we really think to supportive family members, good things usually happen:

- We know our family cares about us.
- We believe our opinions and concerns are important.
- Problems are prevented because they are discussed in advance.
- Several people can help find solutions to problems.
- Our family is closer and stronger because we help one another.

In our efforts to be open and honest, we should always remember to be kind. In the name of honesty sometimes we can easily hurt feelings and weaken relationships. We should be sensitive to the feelings of others as we speak. In the Disney movie *Bambi,* the rabbit Thumper gave wonderful advice: "If you can't say somethin' nice, don't say nothin' at all."

Elder M. Russell Ballard said, "A word to you children: Never be disrespectful to your parents. You must also learn to listen, especially to the counsel of your mom and dad and to the promptings of the Spirit" (*Ensign,* May 1999, 87).

FAMILY SURVEY REVIEW
Statement 12: In our family we can say what we feel.

- Can we say what we really feel in our family?
- What are some of the reasons we don't share our feelings?
- What can we do to help each other "open up?"

STORY

One day, not long before the end of World War II, a young boy in Germany, named Reimund, saw two airmen parachuting out of an enemy plane that had been shot down. Like many other curious citizens who had seen the parachutists falling through the afternoon sky, eleven-year-old Reimund went to the city's central square to wait for the police to arrive with the prisoners of war. Eventually two policemen arrived with two British prisoners in tow. They would wait in the city square for a car to take the British airmen to a prison where prisoners of war were kept.

When the crowd saw the prisoners, there were angry shouts of "Kill them! Kill them!" No doubt they were thinking of the heavy bombings their city had suffered at the hands of the British. Many of the crowd had come from their fields with pitchforks, shovels, and other tools.

Reimund looked at the faces of the British prisoners. They were only nineteen or twenty years old. He could see that they were very frightened. He could also see that the two policemen, whose duty it was to protect the prisoners, were no match for the angry crowd with its pitchforks and shovels.

Reimund knew he had to do something, and he had to do it quickly. He ran to place himself between the prisoners and the crowd, turning to face the crowd and shouting to them to stop. Not wanting to hurt the boy, the crowd held back for a moment, long enough for Reimund to shout, "Look at these prisoners. They are just young boys! They are only doing what your own sons are doing—fighting for their country. If your sons were shot down in a foreign country and became prisoners of war, you wouldn't want the people there to kill your sons. So please don't hurt these boys!"

Reimund's fellow townspeople listened in amazement, then shame. Finally, a woman said, "It took a little boy to tell us what is right and what is wrong." The crowd dispersed.

Reimund has never forgotten the look of tremendous relief and gratitude on the faces of the young British airmen. He hopes they have had long, happy lives, and that they haven't forgotten the little boy who saved them.

—Contributed by Elaine McDonald[55]

Discussion

1. If you were Reimund, would you have done the same thing he did?
2. Do we speak up at home, school, or work for what we know is right or wrong? If no, why don't we speak up?
3. Can anyone tell about a time when he or she spoke up for what was right?

Activity

Family members will all take turns doing this activity. One person asks a question to another family member. The person who answers the question needs to be completely honest, although kind, in his or her response. The two family members should talk to each other in a very open, totally honest way. Listeners should respond only positively. Try to use the skills that were taught in the lessons on listening and positive words.

1. What is something that happened during the last year that made you happy?
2. What is one thing you dislike about yourself?
3. What is one thing that gets you angry?
4. What is one thing you think our family can do to be happier?
5. What do you think you can do to make our family better?

Assignment

As a family participate in one or both of the following Additional Activities: The Talking Box and Correspondence.

ADDITIONAL ACTIVITY

THE TALKING BOX

Parents and children need to keep the lines of communication open, but sometimes it's hard to get conversations started, especially when there are important matters to discuss. This activity can help your family talk to one another about important issues.

ACTIVITY INSTRUCTIONS

1. Set up:
   - Family members prepare the question cards by copying the questions below, cutting the questions apart, and gluing them to index cards. You may want to read the questions ahead of time to see if they are appropriate for the ages of your children. Then put the question cards in the "talking box."
   - Encourage family members to add more questions.

2. Use the Talking Box:
   - Put the box on the table. Allow everyone to choose a question.
   - Take the box on family outings and trips in the car.
   - Discuss the questions during bedtime talks or other appropriate times.

3. Agree to the following rules:
   - Family members may not criticize one another for any comment made during talking box discussions.
   - If people don't want to answer a question, they may choose another one or pass.
   - No one should be pressured into participating in this activity.

TALKING BOX QUESTIONS

For Very Young Children:

- What do you want to be when you are big?
- What would you do if you could stay up all night?
- If you were the mommy or daddy in this family, what would you do when the children act naughty?
- What do you think grown-up people do for fun?

For Elementary School Children:

- What advice would you give parents about raising children?
- What do most children at your school do at recess time?
- What is something you would like to change about your school?
- Why do you think some children are so mean to others?

- Who is your best friend? Why do you like him/her?
- What do you think it is like having you for a son/daughter?

For Teenagers:

- What age would you like to be?
- When you have teenage children of your own, what kind of parent do you think you will be?
- Explain why you agree or disagree with the following statement: "School years are the best years of your life."
- Why do you think some teenagers do drugs?
- What do you think it is like having you for a son/daughter?

For Parents:

- What is something you really enjoy about being a parent?
- What day from your childhood would you want to relive?
- What is something you have learned about life?
- Describe a time you got really angry with your parents as a child.
- What is something you did when you were in high school that you hope your children will not do?
- What do you think it is like having you for a parent?

Other Questions:

- What is something you worry about?
- Describe something that happened recently that made you really happy.
- Describe something people do that makes you really angry.
- If there were going to be an earthquake tomorrow and your family had to move out of your house, what would you want to take with you?
- If you could spend an afternoon with a famous person (living or dead), who would you choose and why?
- Do you think it is ever right to tell a lie?
- Why do you think some children run away from home?
- Explain your feelings about divorce.
- What do you think happens to people after death?
- Why do you think some people tell jokes about people who belong to different races, religions, or nationalities?

ADDITIONAL ACTIVITIES
CORRESPONDENCE

Friends and relatives who live in other places enjoy hearing about what's happening in our family. However, sometimes the days and weeks go by so quickly that we don't always stay in touch with them. The two activities below are to help families correspond with one another in creative ways.

ACTIVITY 1 INSTRUCTIONS

1. Address a large envelope to a relative who lives far away.

2. Keep the envelope in a place that is easy to reach (bulletin board or refrigerator).

3. Fill the envelope with the things that reflect what family members have been doing. If necessary, write a note on items to explain them.

- Completed homework assignments and quizzes
- Drawings, pages from coloring books, and other "original art"
- Notes from teachers
- Programs, agendas, or schedules from meetings, music recitals, concerts, school plays, and other events
- Ticket stubs
- Newspaper clippings
- Recipes
- Photos

4. After a week, or when the envelope is filled, mail it to a relative.

5. Address a new envelope to another family member and start again.

The following activity is designed to help your family get into the letter-writing habit so you can stay close to loved ones.

ACTIVITY 2 INSTRUCTIONS

1. Assemble the following supplies in a box: paper, pens, pencils, envelopes, and stamps.

2. Talk to your family about why it is important to write to friends and relatives.

3. Explain that any time someone has a letter to write, all the supplies can be found in one place. Always keep the writing supplies in the box so you won't have to hunt for them.

4. Consider setting aside half an hour each month for a family "write-in." Everybody chooses a different relative or friend to write to. Then all letters are passed around the table for everyone to add a short note.

5. Use the form letter included after Lesson Seven if you can't think of anything to say.

6. Replenish supplies on a regular basis.

SOLUTIONS THROUGH STORIES AND POEMS: COMMUNICATION

COMMUNICATE BY EXAMPLE

Michael J. Dowling was a young man who fell from a wagon in a blizzard in Michigan when he was fourteen years of age. Before his parents discovered that he had fallen from the rear of the wagon, he had been frostbitten. His right leg was amputated almost to the hip, his left leg above the knee; his right arm was amputated; [and] his left hand was amputated. Not much future for a young lad like that, was there? Do you know what he did? He went to the board of county commissioners and he told them that if they would educate him he would pay back every penny.

During World War I, Mr. Dowling, who was at the time president of one of the largest banks in St. Paul, went to Europe to visit the soldiers—to visit those who were wounded. . . . Upon one occasion he was in a large hotel in London, and he had before him the wounded soldiers in their wheelchairs. They were in a lobby, and he was up on the mezzanine floor. As he started to speak, he minimized the seriousness of their wounds; the fact that one had lost an eye, another had lost an arm, etc., were no grounds for complaint. And he got these fellows so wrought up that they started to boo him. Then he walked over to the stairway and down the stairs toward the lobby, telling them as he walked how fortunate they were, and they continued booing.

Finally, he sat down on one of the steps and took off his right leg. And he kept on talking and telling them how well off they were. Well, they calmed down a little bit, but they still resented his remarks. Then he took off his left leg. Well, the booing stopped then. But before he arrived at the bottom of the stairs, he had taken off his right arm and flipped off his left hand, and there he sat—just the stump of a body.

Michael Dowling was the president of one of the biggest banks in St. Paul. He had married and was the father of five children. Mr. Dowling contributed greatly to bettering others' lives, and most significantly in encouraging the wounded soldiers of World War I.

—Contributed by Matthew Cowley[56]

If you treat a man as he is, he will stay as he is, but if you treat him as if he were what he ought to be, and could be, he will be that bigger and better man.

—Goethe[57]

THOUGHTS

A few months after moving to a small town a woman complained to a neighbor about the poor service at the local drugstore. She hoped the new acquaintance would repeat her complaint to the owner.

The next time she went to the drugstore, the druggist greeted her with a big smile and told her how happy he was to see her again. He said he hoped she liked their town and to please let him know if there was anything he could do to help her and her husband get settled. He then filled her order promptly and efficiently.

Later the woman reported the miraculous change to her friend. "I suppose you told the druggist how poor I thought the service was?" she asked.

"Well, no," the woman said. "In fact—and I hope you don't mind—I told him you were amazed at the way he had built up this small-town drugstore and that you thought it was one of the best run drugstores you'd ever seen."

—Author Unknown[58]

IT SHOWS IN YOUR FACE

You don't have to tell how you live each day,
You don't have to say if you work or play,
A tried, true barometer serves in your place;
However you live, it will show in your face.
The false, the deceit that you bear in your heart
Will not stay inside, where it first got a start,
For sinew and blood are a thin veil of lace;
What you wear in your heart you wear in your face.
If your life is unselfish, if for others you live
For not what you get, but for what you can give,
If you live close to God, in His infinite grace,
You don't have to tell it; it shows in your face.

—Author Unknown[59]

SCATTER SUNSHINE

Oh, scatter sunshine as you go
In all you say and do;
The love and kindness which you show
Will come right back to you!

There is an unseen register
Where all your deeds are filled;
The times you stopped to lend a hand,
The times you paused and smiled.
The times you spoke a fitting word
Of joy and comfort, too;
The times you went the second mile
Some gracious deed to do;

The times you quietly withstood
An enemy's sharp blow,
The times you opened wide your heart
And let the merry flow;
The ways in which you remembered
Some token small to share;
The times you took a moment out
To breathe a silent prayer;

Like homing pigeons they'll return
To bring you gladness, too . . .

These rays of sunshine, warm and bright
Will come right back to you!

—Contributed by Lois Rasmussen[60]

KEYS

Hearts, like doors, will open with ease
To very, very little keys;
And don't forget that two of these
Are "I thank you" and "If you please."

—Author Unknown[61]

I KNOW SOMETHING GOOD ABOUT YOU

Wouldn't this old world be better,
If the folks we meet would say—
"I know something good about you!"
And then treat us just that way?

Wouldn't it be fine and dandy
If each handclasp, fond and true,
Carried with it this assurance—
"I know something good about you!"

Wouldn't life be lots more happy
If the good that's in us all
Were the only thing about us
That folks bothered to recall?

Wouldn't life be lots more happy
If we praised the good we see?
For there's such a lot of goodness
In the worst of you and me!

Wouldn't it be nice to practice
That fine way of thinking, too?
You know something good about me,
I know something good about you.

—Author Unknown[62]

WORTH WHILE

It is easy enough to be pleasant
When life flows by like a song,
But the man worth while is one who will smile
When everything goes dead wrong.
For the test of the heart is trouble,

And it always comes with the years,
And the smile that is worth the praises of earth
Is the smile that shines through tears.

It is easy enough to be prudent,
When nothing tempts you to stray,
When without or within no voice of sin
Is luring your soul away;
But it's only a negative virtue
Until it is tried by fire,
And the life that is worth the honor of earth
Is the life that resists desire.

By the cynic, the sad, the fallen,
Who had no strength for the strife,
The world's highway is cumbered today;
They make up the item of life.
But the virtue that conquers passion,
And the sorrow that hides in a smile,
It is these that are worth the homage of earth,
For we find them but once in a while.

—Contributed by Ella Wheeler Wilcox[63]

Chapter Four
Choices Solution

*Choose you this day whom you will serve . . . but as for me and
my house, we will serve the Lord.*

—Joshua 24:15

Introduction for Parents

Let's talk about a concept that can be absolutely life-changing—choice. Back in the year A.D. 150, Marcus Aurelius, a philosopher and writer, said, "Reject your sense of injury and the injury itself disappears."[64]

We can choose to be unhappy and take offense, or we can choose to be happy and forgiving. Abraham Lincoln understood this. He said, "Most people are about as happy as they make up their mind to be."[65]

Dale Carnegie understood this also. He said, "Happiness doesn't depend on outward conditions. It depends on inner conditions. It isn't what you have or who you are or where you are or what you are doing that makes you happy or unhappy. It is what you think about it. For example, two people may be in the same place, doing the same thing; both may have about an equal amount of money and prestige—and yet one may be miserable and the other happy. Why? Because of a different mental attitude."[66]

When we understand this fully, we no longer say, "He *makes* me angry" because no one makes you angry—it's a choice! And we don't blame others, or our circumstances, or the past for our unhappiness.

Imagine for a moment that the year is 1945, and you are in Auschwitz, Germany. You're imprisoned in a concentration camp whose horror defies description. Your entire family has been killed. The guards have stripped you, beaten you, starved you, and deprived you of sleep. Viktor Frankl, a Jewish psychiatrist, experienced all of this. But as he was experiencing this hell on earth, he came to an incredible understanding. It was this: the guards could torture him, but he had the power to respond to them however he chose. They could beat him, but they couldn't take away his will to live. They could strip him, but he could clothe himself with mental power beyond their reach. They could starve him, but he could feast on his dreams of the future. Viktor Frankl imagined himself at the pulpits of many universities, teaching future generations about the ultimate freedom—the freedom to choose how you respond to life.[67]

How do we choose to respond to life? Let's talk about a choice and a concern that we all share in common: controlling our thoughts.

Except when we're in the deepest sleep cycle, we're always thinking. Even now, as you're reading, you're thinking and relating everything to your personal life experiences. Some of our thoughts are positive and productive, and others are negative, fearful, or worrisome. The important question isn't whether or not we're going to have negative thoughts—we are! It's what we *choose* to do with the ones we have. We can overanalyze them and obsess about them, or we can refuse to be pulled down by them. The truth is, we *can* dismiss negative thoughts. Is it easy? Sometimes. Is it possible? Always.

When you have a thought, that's all it is—a thought! It can't hurt you without your permission. For example, if you have a thought from your past like, "I'm upset because my father made so many mistakes. He really messed me up. How can I be expected to be a good father when I had a lousy example?" you can let that thought go round and round in your mind, allowing it to pull you down. You can convince yourself that because of your dad you're a C+ father to your kids.

Or, you can choose to control your thoughts. This doesn't mean your father didn't make your childhood difficult—he may have—but you're not there anymore. *Now* you can either let his failures affect you negatively or learn from them and be a better father; more aware of what *not* to do.

Additionally, controlling your thoughts can help resolve arguments. A disagreement you may have had this morning as you were leaving the house, or last week, or last year, no longer exists as an actual argument. It exists only as a thought in your mind. You can either dwell on it or refuse to let it affect you negatively.

When you are able to control your thoughts, you can control your words and actions too, because every word and action begins with a thought. I'll give you the secret of how to control every thought. There are two easy steps:

1. *Whenever a negative thought enters your mind, label it.* Say to yourself, "That was negative, and that's not like me. I'm usually positive." When you think this way, you're stopping the negative thought and defining yourself as a positive person. As you do this over and over, you'll become a positive person who very rarely thinks negative thoughts.

2. *Replace the negative thought with a positive one.* For example, lets say you pull up to a gorgeous person driving a beautiful new car. Your immediate thought might be, "Wow, look at her. I'll never look as good as that!" The instant you think that way, say to yourself, "That was negative, and that's not like me. I'm usually positive." Then replace the negative thought with a positive one. Say to yourself, "Look at her. She looks great! And that's a beautiful car!"

Why do we compare ourselves with others? We shouldn't! Other people's possessions or talents don't reflect on us. We should try to rejoice when others rejoice, and be happy for them. Comparing is a bad habit that leads to jealousy and discouragement.

Remember, these are choices. We can respond to every life situation exactly how we choose.

Now, what if it's hard for you to break the habit of comparing yourself with other people, or criticizing, or any other bad habit? In Ether we can read the Lord's promise to us if we're trying our best to change and we're having difficulty: "For if they humble themselves before me, and have faith in me, then will I make weak things become strong unto them" (Ether 12:27).

How do we teach our children to make wise choices? By example. We need to live the principles in which we believe, and our children will usually follow in our footsteps.

Elder M. Russell Ballard wrote, "Just as it is difficult for a weary sailor to find his way across uncharted seas without the aid of a compass, it is almost impossible for children and youth to find their way through the seas of life without the guiding light of a good example. We cannot expect them to avoid those things that are inappropriate if they see their parents compromising principles and failing to live the gospel" (*Ensign,* May 1999, 87).

A second way that we can teach our children to make wise choices is to teach them correct principles and then provide them opportunities to make choices. When our children are about two years old we can give them choices in small things. Allowing children to make decisions, even about how high to pour milk in a glass, helps them become responsible and choose more wisely as they get older.

Making decisions is a fundamental life skill, and our children need lots of practice. Young people who haven't made decisions about who they are and what they want to do in life are the most vulnerable to peer pressure. Inexperienced decision makers are more likely to rely on others to make their decisions and define their values for them. On the other hand, experienced decision makers become mature teenagers and adults who are able to stand up for what they know is right. They can do this because they've thought problems through, made many decisions, and learned for themselves what works and what doesn't.

Of course, decisions children make, especially as teenagers, should be choices within limits; choices between things that parents approve of. For example, from the time children are very young they should hear, "You can't play in the street, but you can play in the backyard or in the house." Or, "It's almost time for bed. Would you rather get ready for bed now and then read until it's sleep time, or would you like to play a board game and then get ready for bed?"

As children grow, they can be given more and more responsibility and greater opportunity to make their own decisions, always within parental limits. Accountability goes hand in hand with choice. We teach accountability every time our children experience the consequences, either good or bad, for the decisions they make.

If good choices are made, the child earns our trust and is given more privileges. If bad choices are made, the child loses our trust and privileges are taken away. Parents need to talk about this clearly so children understand this point. We handicap our children when we don't require them to be accountable for their choices.

One of the greatest lessons our Heavenly Father taught Adam and Eve was a lesson on choice and accountability. Consider the instruction given to Adam by the Lord: "Of every tree of the garden thou mayest freely eat: But of the tree of the knowledge of good and evil, thou shalt not eat of it: for in the day that thou eatest thereof thou shalt surely die" (Gen. 2:16–17).

First, the Lord was instructive: He began with a statement of what Adam could do: "Of every tree of the garden thou mayest freely eat." Second, He told Adam what was expected of him. Third, He clearly stated the consequences. It was a consequence Adam would bring upon himself by the choice he made.

There is a parenting model here:

1. Parents must first teach children what they can do.
2. Parents state their expectations of children.
3. Parents clearly state the consequences that can/will be "earned."
4. Parents allow children to make choices.
5. Parents let the consequences of these choices teach children.

Now let's take a real-life example and apply this model: Mom had a doctor's appointment and wouldn't be there after school when fifteen-year-old Jacob came home.

1. Jacob was told that after school he could shoot hoops with his friend after he took out the trash and fed the dog.
2. Mom told Jacob that she expected him to do his two chores immediately when he got home.
3. Mom explained that if Jacob did his chores before playing basketball, he could play the next day also. If he didn't do his chores first, he couldn't shoot hoops the following day.
4. As soon as Jacob got off the bus from school, he went straight to his friend's home to play basketball.

5. When Jacob's mom returned, she simply said, "I'm sorry you chose the wrong today, son. Now you won't be able to shoot hoops tomorrow." When Jacob began to whine and complain, she just said, "I'm sure you'll make a better choice next time."

Two things helped make this a learning experience:

1. There was extreme clarity on each point; Jacob couldn't possibly misunderstand his mother.
2. Mom was in total control. There was no yelling, just a calm explanation of the consequences of his choice.

The challenge is allowing children to learn hard lessons by exercising their agency. But note the importance of this principle: If children use their agency to make good choices, they'll enjoy the positive consequences, which will lead to more good choices. Then making good decisions becomes their comfort zone, and choosing the right becomes habitual. Parents, this is what we want! Let's make choices each day that will draw us closer to our Heavenly Father and to our loved ones.

Lesson Thirteen

Responsibility

The responsibility for each member's social, emotional, spiritual, physical, or economic well-being rests first upon himself, second upon his family, and third upon the Church.

—President Spencer W. Kimball (*Ensign*, Aug. 1984, 4)

FOLLOW-UP

(As a family, discuss the assignment for the lesson "Open Communication.")

1. Have we been sharing our feelings with family members in a more open way? How? When?
2. How have we been more kind and understanding when family members try to communicate openly and honestly?

CONCEPT

One of the most important things we can learn in this life is to take responsibility for our own thoughts, words, and actions. When we do this, we don't let other people make us angry. We wouldn't say, "You make me angry!" because no one *makes* us angry. We choose to be annoyed or to be cheerful. We choose to be angry and out of control or to remain calm and in control of our emotions, no matter what is happening around us.

When we're responsible, we no longer blame others, the weather, or our memory. For example, we wouldn't say things like, "It's not my fault. I forgot!" If something goes wrong, we can explain, but we make no excuses. If we make a mistake, we take responsibility for it. We admit when we're wrong.

Linda Kavelin Papov, in her book *The Family Virtues Guide*, described responsibility well: "Being responsible means that others can depend on you. Being responsible means to do something well and to the best of your ability. Being responsible is being willing to be accountable for what you do or not . . . You accept credit when you do things right (humbly, of course!), and you accept correction when things go wrong. When you are responsible, you keep your agreements. If you agree to do something for your family or for a friend, you don't put it off or forget about it. You make sure it gets done. Being responsible is the ability to respond ably."[68]

Additionally, children learn responsibility by doing as much as possible for themselves. As young children accomplish even the smallest things, older children and parents should praise them. Parents, the fewer things we do *for* our children, the more time we'll have to do things *with* them.

President Gordon B. Hinckley taught, "Children need to work with their parents, to wash dishes with them, to mop floors with them, to mow lawns, to prune trees and shrubbery, to paint and fix up, to clean up, and do a hundred other things in which they will learn that labor is the price of cleanliness, progress, and prosperity" (*Ensign,* Sep. 1996, 7).

The famous inventor Thomas Edison said, "I never did anything worth doing by accident, nor did any of my inventions come by accident. They came by work."[69]

FAMILY SURVEY REVIEW
Statement 13: We take responsibility for our own mistakes.

- When something goes wrong, is it easy to blame others? Why?
- Instead of blaming others, what should we say and do?

STORY

Relate this fictionalized story to open a family discussion:

Just over the six-foot fence in Jason's backyard was a parking lot for an apartment building. Someone had tossed a paper bag of empty beer bottles from the parking lot over the fence into Jason's backyard where he had found them. Jason took the bottles and tossed them, one by one, back over the fence. Since he couldn't see through the fence, he couldn't see them land, but he could hear the crash each time a bottle broke in the parking lot. It was kind of fun.

That evening a man from the apartments rang the doorbell, and Jason, who was downstairs, overheard the man telling his father about a punctured tire. Jason went quietly into his room, quickly put on his pajamas, got in bed, and pretended to be asleep.

His parents, after reassuring the neighbor they would pay for the tire if it turned out to be their son's doing, sat down to decide how to handle the incident. They realized that they had three challenges: (1) to help Jason tell the truth about the matter (they knew him well enough to be pretty sure what the truth was); (2) to help him feel sorry for what he'd done; and (3) to help him feel enough responsibility for his actions that he wouldn't do something similarly irresponsible in the future. As they thought about it, they realized that it was fortunate the whole thing had come to their attention after Jason was in bed, when they had time to think it through alone rather than in his presence. Otherwise, they might have confronted him without turning it into a learning experience.

When Jason came to breakfast the next morning, Dad said, "Son, I noticed that sack of beer bottles. Whoever tossed them into our yard shouldn't have done it, should he?"

Jason looked up with a little hope in his eyes and answered, "No."

Dad said, "You probably felt like tossing them back over and didn't really stop to think that they might hurt someone or break something." Jason looked down, but said nothing. "Did you throw them over, son?"

There was a pause, then a quiet, "Yes."

"We're proud of you for telling the truth, son. A man's car ran over one of those bottles and got a flat tire. We're lucky none of the bottles broke a windshield. But we do need to decide what to do about that flat tire. Do you feel sorry about throwing those bottles and puncturing the tire?"

"Yes."

"Are you going to take responsibility for what you did?"

"Yes."

Jason cleaned up the rest of the glass. He saved money from working for three weeks to pay for the tire. He apologized to the car's owner. He promised both his parents and the car owner that he would never throw anything over the fence again. Jason made restitution and took responsibility for his actions.

DISCUSSION

1. How did Jason take responsibility for his actions?
2. How do we feel when we take responsibility for our words and actions?

ACTIVITY

First, we'll answer the following questions. They'll help us realize that our daily decisions show how responsible we are:

1. What would you do if you broke something in our home?
2. What if you had a family job to do, and your friend asked you to go swimming?
3. What if your teacher gave you a math assignment that you didn't understand and it was to be finished the next day—what would you do?
4. What if you were tending a neighbor's child who was in the bathtub when the phone rang?

Second, we'll do one (or both) of the activities on the following pages:

1. Ten-Minute Pickup
2. The Honey-Do Jar

ASSIGNMENT

1. During the coming weeks make a special effort to take responsibility for your own thoughts, words, and actions.
2. Read the Additional Solution for Success included with this lesson: Learning to Make Responsible Decisions.

ACTIVITY

THE TEN-MINUTE PICKUP

All family members have a responsibility to keep the home clean. The following activity is a fun way for family members to combine their energies, get household chores done faster, and feel good about doing their part.

ACTIVITY INSTRUCTIONS

1. Assign family members to "work stations" (areas of the house that need cleaning).
2. Be sure everyone has what they need for cleaning—vacuum cleaner, broom, sponge, etc.
3. Set the timer for ten or fifteen minutes and shout, "On your mark, get set, CLEAN!"
4. Family members are to work quickly and efficiently at their stations to get as much done as possible before the buzzer goes off. If someone finishes early, he or she should run to another station and help someone else.
5. As soon as time is up, allow a few moments for any last-minute cleaning. Then stand back and join in a round of applause for everyone who helped accomplish a marvelous job in such a short time!

ACTIVITY

HONEY-DO JAR

Dividing household chores among all family members is a good way for children to learn responsibility. This activity guarantees that children will have a chance to do every chore at least once. This is a fair way to distribute housekeeping responsibilities and a good way to prepare children to be on their own someday.

1. Schedule a family meeting to:
   - Make a list of chores (inside and out) that family members can do.
   - Put a D next to daily chores.
   - Put a W next to weekly chores.
   - Put an M next to monthly chores.

2. Cut construction paper into "chore strips." Write one chore per strip as follows:
   - Red strips have daily chores.
   - Green strips have weekly chores.
   - Blue strips have monthly chores.

3. Put chore strips into the "Honey-Do" jar.

4. Decide how many chore strips, and what color, each family member should draw. These decisions will be determined by family members' ages and abilities.

5. Have family members draw from the Honey-Do jar at the beginning of every month.

6. Make sure that the more time-consuming and strenuous chores are distributed fairly.

7. Make a separate Honey-Do jar filled with easier tasks for very young children, like folding towels, pulling weeds, and picking up toys.

8. For one month, family members perform the chores they drew from the jar. Repeat the drawing each month.

ADDITIONAL SOLUTION FOR SUCCESS

LEARNING TO MAKE RESPONSIBLE DECISIONS

Suppose we wanted to take a trip. What would be the best way to get there? Choosing a route is a lot like the process we go through when we make any decision. We should consider many possible routes or solutions. Next, we should look at the benefits and costs of each alternative way in terms of time, comfort, cost, scenery, etc. We will then be able to choose the route that will best meet our needs. Similarly, when we make any meaningful decision, we should consider several solutions, then make our best choice based on the information we have. There are usually a number of ways we can accomplish things. Making good decisions is the process of identifying the one way that will work best for us.

After we've given all possible solutions careful thought and we've made our best decision, we should not look back with regret. Later, if our decision proves to be the wrong one, we should remember that we made the best decision we could with the information we had at the time.

THE DECISION-MAKING PROCESS

1. Identify the problem.
2. List all possible solutions.
3. Think about each alternative, applying your knowledge, values, and resources.
4. Discuss the issue with those who care about your welfare and happiness. If appropriate, make it a matter of prayer.
5. Choose the best solution.

Keep in mind that decision making doesn't always mean that there is one "right" choice. Different people may choose different, but equally successful, ways to solve problems.

ACTIVITY

Three problem situations are found below. After thinking about the five steps of decision making listed above, make a decision about what you would do in each situation, and tell why you would solve the problem that way.

Problem 1: Friday night is the big game with your school's rival team. It is also your cousin's wedding. You want to go to both. What should you do?

Problem 2: You have $25. You see the perfect sweater and you want it. Your mother's birthday is next week. You don't have enough money to buy a gift and the sweater. What should you do?

Problem 3: You have been asked to join the track team for spring season. You also want to be in the school play. Both play rehearsal and team practice are after school. What should you do?

Family members are more likely to include one another in their important decisions if they are listened to and feel as if their family cares. Criticizing a family member's decision-making efforts weakens relationships and prevents good communication.

As children grow older and mature, they need to take more and more responsibility for their own decisions. In decisions about college, careers, military service, or even marriage, the primary responsibility ultimately belongs to the young person. A parent can become a trusted advisor and facilitator, helping to locate resources and information so the young person can make informed decisions.

In most families, children grow to young adulthood making decisions that are generally in harmony with their parents' beliefs and values. Sometimes children will choose otherwise. For many parents it is a challenge to continue to accept, support, and love their child despite their differences. However, loving as Christ loves will enable a rich relationship to continue throughout life for both parent and child.

Lesson Fourteen
Rules and Consequences

While we are free to choose, once we have made those choices, we are tied to the consequences of our choices.
—Elder Russell M. Nelson (*Ensign*, Nov. 1988, 7)

FOLLOW-UP

(As a family, discuss the assignment for the lesson "Responsibility.")

1. How have we improved in our efforts to take responsibility for our own thoughts, words, and actions?
2. Do we blame others less?
3. Are we eliminating excuses? Can anyone tell us about a time they didn't make an excuse for something they did wrong?

CONCEPT

In life there are rules—at home, at school, and in the community. It's important to have rules in a family for order and peace to exist. When all family members help make the rules, children take the responsibility of helping to set their own limits. Families should gather together and decide on family rules that need to be obeyed by all family members.

A consequence is the result of a choice. When rules are obeyed, good consequences usually follow. When rules are disobeyed, unpleasant consequences follow.

Elder Joseph B. Wirthlin declared, "With absolute certainty, choices of good and right lead to happiness and peace, while choices of sin and evil eventually lead to unhappiness, sorrow, and misery" (*Ensign,* Nov. 1989, 75).

After creating family rules, everyone can decide on the consequences for disobedience. To best change behavior, whenever possible, the consequence should relate to the rule that was disobeyed.

Example: A child disobeys and returns home late after dinner is over. Possible consequences are that he fixes his own dinner or waits until morning to eat.

Example: A child forgets to take his homework to school. A possible consequence is that he receives a lower grade, then he does extra-credit work to raise his grade.

Consequences can be used inappropriately. For example, if a student's grades are unacceptable, and the consequence is removal from the one school activity that the student likes, then he may have even less desire to go to school. It would be more appropriate to have the consequence for falling grades be extra study time in the evening, under parental supervision. When deciding on rules and consequences as a family, be careful to make them reasonable and "do-able."

When children help create family rules and consequences and then disobey, they are disobeying rules they once agreed upon. Then parents can simply empathize with their children's bad decisions and remind them of the previously agreed-upon consequence that they'll now experience because of their wrong choices.

When it becomes necessary for parents to enforce rules and consequences, it is best to be kind and firm at the same time. Gentle words and loving actions show kindness. Consistent follow-through with appropriate consequences shows firmness. An example of firmness is, "I'm willing to have Jerry stay overnight only if both of you agree to go to bed by ten o'clock." There needs to be appropriate follow-through if the children disobey. This could mean that the parents take Jerry home or he isn't allowed to spend the night again.

It is important to understand that obedience to family rules prepares children for life outside the home and brings a greater measure of peace and happiness inside the home.

Elder Bruce R. McConkie reminds us, "Obedience is the first law of heaven, the cornerstone upon which all righteousness and progression rest."[70]

FAMILY SURVEY REVIEW
Statement 14: We all help make the rules in our family.

- Children, do you like the idea of helping to make the rules?
- Will it be easier to obey rules that you helped make? Why?
- What should consequences teach us?

STORY

The Canadian Northlands have only two seasons, winter and July. As the backroads begin to thaw, they become muddy and vehicles traveling through the backcountry leave deep ruts. The ground freezes hard during the winter months, and the highway ruts become a part of the traveling challenges. For vehicles entering this undeveloped area during the winter, there is a sign which reads, "Driver, please choose carefully which rut you drive in, because you'll be in it for the next 20 miles." Choose carefully the path your life takes. Once you choose, your choices will control you.[71]

It will be difficult to get out of your "ruts." There are consequences in life for the choices we make.

Discussion

1. What are some rules at school? at work? in the community?
2. What happens when those rules are broken?
3. Are people usually happier when they obey the rules?

Activity

With everyone helping, we're going to create some family rules. Then we'll decide on consequences for obedience or disobedience to the rules.

1. Have one person write down all ideas suggested.
2. Let everyone have a chance to share his or her ideas about what would be good rules for your family.
3. Remember to keep your rules few and simple.

Example: One family member may say, "I think we should have a rule of no hitting in our family." We'll write that down. Then someone might say, "We should each keep our bedroom clean." We will get everyone's ideas for rules. Then we'll talk about which ideas should become our family rules.

Now let's make a list of our family rules and display them somewhere in our home. Then let's discuss the consequences for obeying our family rules.

Example: The consequence for not hitting one another is helping to create peace and a loving atmosphere in our home. A consequence for keeping bedrooms clean is a tidy home that contributes to family peace, order, and well-being.

Next, let's decide on the consequences for disobeying the rules.

> *Example:* A consequence for hitting would be to apologize then to go away from the family for a few minutes to think about being kind next time. A possible consequence for not keeping a bedroom clean is staying in the messy room and not participating in enjoyable activities until the room is clean.

ASSIGNMENT

1. Make a real effort to obey your family rules and to have good attitudes when dealing with a consequence. Parents, try to be loving, firm, and consistent.
2. Read the Additional Solution for Success: Family Values.

ADDITIONAL SOLUTION FOR SUCCESS

FAMILY VALUES

Each of us lives by a set of values that guides our behavior, helps us make decisions, and tells us what is right and wrong. We display our values every day by the way we speak and act. For example, the way we use our time and how we spend our money both reveal what we value.

"My son just doesn't have any values," complained an annoyed father.

"Well," said his friend, "just what are your family's values?"

"Ah, ummm, well, uhh . . ." the first man stammered. "I guess I just haven't thought about it that way."[72]

Often we haven't really thought about our values or why people believe and act differently than we do. Discussing with others the differences in our beliefs can help us understand one another. Understanding our differences can promote a healthy tolerance for other people.

The rules we have in our families are a result of our values—the things we think are really important. It's vital that everyone know the difference between what's really important and what doesn't matter too much. Is not getting a haircut as important as not going to school? What can be negotiated and what can't?

It is possible to be flexible and still firmly based in solid values. The key is to distinguish between values that are negotiable (and can be decided by family members on their own) and those that aren't. There are certain issues that require absolute obedience. President Abraham Lincoln said in his last public address, "Important principles may, and must, be inflexible."[73] These inflexible rules need to be clearly defined and understood by all family members. On less important issues family members may choose for themselves. Many families quarrel about things that aren't on the "really important" list, and parents spend time being irritated unnecessarily. First parents, then families together, need to decide on important rules that must be obeyed and then, "Don't sweat the small stuff."

Today people sometimes avoid declaring right from wrong. "After all," they say, "everyone has the right to their own ideas, and who is to say that parents should impose their thinking on their children?" Parents may argue that they don't want to require a lot of "do's" and "don'ts." However, families who do not teach moral values deprive their children of a solid basis for approaching life. Children want and need boundaries. They need to be taught that in life there are principles of truth, which, if lived, will bring happiness. If those principles, or moral values, are not a part of your life, the consequence is unhappiness. People in strong families are not afraid to talk about values. They don't crumble if not everyone agrees with their point of view. They know where they stand, and they're willing to be recognized for it.

Children from such families are able to move into society and do what they know is right, not just what others say they should. The more candid the discussion of values in the home, the better prepared family members are to hold to these values when they are challenged. If decisions are made not just on the basis of what is easiest, cheapest, or fastest, but what is the right thing to do, children develop a higher sense of moral behavior. Such children would not have the same fuzzy thinking of a college student, for example, who explained that he had stolen a bike "because it wasn't locked."[74] To this student his behavior was the fault of someone else. When people behave according to a set of clear standards, their sense of self-worth and self-respect is elevated. We define ourselves by our values.

Of course, the most important way to teach good moral values is by the example set in the home. Albert Schweitzer said, "There are three ways to effectively teach a child. First is example, and second is by example, and third is through example."[75]

As Elder H. Burke Peterson put it, "If our words are not consistent with our actions, they will never be heard above the thunder of our deeds" (*Ensign,* Nov. 1992, 43). We need to live the values we believe.

Lesson Fifteen
Problem Prevention

Oh let us think and live and teach the power of prevention.
—Elder Richard L. Evans (*Ensign*, June 1971, 73)

FOLLOW-UP

(As a family, discuss the assignment for the lesson "Rules and Consequences.")

1. How do we feel about our family rules?
2. How do we feel about the consequences to the rules?
3. Are we following through and applying consequences for disobedience? How are our attitudes?

CONCEPT

To avoid conflicts, families should do all they can to prevent problems before they occur. Rather than wait until a conflict arises, it is always better to anticipate it and avoid it.

There are several ways we can help prevent problems:

1. Use a kind tone of voice when speaking.
2. Communicate our feelings and let people know how they can help us.
3. Avoid sarcastic humor and eliminate criticism.
4. Try to sense how a family member is feeling and carefully speak or act in a way that will help them.
5. Keep an open mind and consider the ideas and suggestions of others. Don't be defensive.
6. Give one another high, positive expectations for behavior.

Example of Parent to Child: "I know that as soon as you're finished eating, you'll start doing your homework."

Example of Child to Parent: "I'm sure you'll try to understand what I have to say."

7. Think through and discuss possible problem situations before they happen.
   Example: Ask, "What if a stranger asked to take you home?"
   Example: Ask, "What if an older student pushed you at school?"
8. Keep a sense of humor, and, again, don't sweat the small stuff.
9. Keep the Lord's commandments and follow the counsel of our inspired leaders.
10. Pray earnestly and regularly for divine guidance in your life.

Talking about things that might occur helps us make decisions in advance. Then when the time comes to make a similar decision, we will have thought it through and will choose more wisely. Preventing a problem is usually easier, and more desirable, than trying to solve a problem.

President Spencer W. Kimball remarked, "May I remind all of us that if we will live the gospel and follow the counsel of the leaders of the Church, we will be blessed to avoid many of the problems that plague the world. The Lord knows the challenges we face. If we keep his commandments, we will be entitled to the wisdom and blessings of heaven in solving them" *Ensign,* May 1980, 92).

FAMILY SURVEY REVIEW
Statement 15: We try to prevent problems before they occur.

- When we see something that might become a problem, how do we try to prevent it?
- How can we improve in preventing family problems?

STORY

For years an old farmer plowed around a large rock in his field. The times he hit the rock by mistake resulted in one broken cultivator and two broken plowshares. Each time he approached the rock, he worried about how much crop land he was losing because of it, and he resented the damage it had done to his equipment.

One day he decided he had suffered enough, and the farmer set out to dig the rock up and be done with it. Putting a large crowbar under one side, he found to his surprise that the rock was less than a foot deep in the ground. Soon he had it in his wagon and was carrying it away. The farmer smiled as he thought about how that "big" old rock had caused him so many years of needless problems.[76]

DISCUSSION

1. How could the old farmer have prevented breaking his farm equipment?
2. Are we sometimes like the farmer? With just a little effort, can we avoid some of our problems? How can we do this?
3. How can talking with a caring person help prevent problems sometimes?

ACTIVITY

For our activity we're going to play the "What If?" game. We can use the questions in the lesson, or we can make up our own. Questions asked should be ones that can help us prevent possible problems. (Everyone should participate in answering the questions.)

1. What if a fire started in the home while you were alone?
2. What if you were at a party when people started doing things you thought were wrong?
3. What if you were tending someone's child when he cut himself badly?
4. What if you were taking a test at school when the student behind you asked for an answer?
5. What if you were at a friend's house and, when it was time to go home, the movie you were watching wasn't finished?

ASSIGNMENT

Choose one or both of the following assignments:
1. Read the Additional Solution for Success: Choices That Prevent and Solve Problems.
2. Read the Additional Solution for Success: Coping with Family Stress.

ADDITIONAL SOLUTION FOR SUCCESS
CHOICES THAT PREVENT AND SOLVE PROBLEMS

- **Simplify Your Life.** It's easy to get too busy. Whenever possible, eliminate activities that complicate your life. Choose the most important things and concentrate on them. Simplify your life.

- **Keep Things in Perspective.** Problems are a normal part of life. Remember that every one has problems. Occasionally ask yourself, "Will this really matter in ten years?" Keep a long-term perspective on life and your problems.

- **Rid Yourself of Worries.** Worry weakens your energy. It reduces your ability to func tion well. Do something about the things that worry you. If you can't do anything about a problem, worrying won't make it better. When you wake up each morning, set goals you can reach that day. Do your best, then don't worry about things you can't do.

- **Live Outside of Yourself.** Helping others and providing support for others is a good way to forget your own problems. Develop friendships and positive relationships out side of your family. Love and care for people, animals, and the environment. Living outside of yourself will bring you great joy.

- **Enjoy Nature as a Family.** Many families find outdoor activities refreshing. There is something special and rejuvenating about being out in nature. Try walks, picnics, campouts, zoos, fishing trips, or outdoor sports. Exercise is very beneficial to your well-being. Develop exercise habits you can enjoy as a family.

- **Develop a Sense of Humor.** Humor can drive away stress and worry. Humor can also prevent problems in remarkable ways. Being able to laugh at some of the things that happen to us keeps life in perspective. Humor lightens loads and helps people relax. Laugh at yourself and laugh with others. Find the humor in your life.

ADDITIONAL SOLUTION FOR SUCCESS

COPING WITH FAMILY STRESS

We have heard much in recent years about how stress affects individuals. It can lead to health problems, emotional problems, and decreased productivity. Stress can cause some family members to get angry or depressed. However, there are healthy ways for family members to cope with stress so that they don't feel overwhelmed. A key to successfully dealing with stress is to develop confidence in your ability to overcome life's challenges.

In the book *Secrets of Strong Families,* Stinnet and DeFrain have identified some coping skills that healthy families have in common. Not all families use every skill, but, in their nationwide study of three thousand families, Stinnet and DeFrain identify six keys to coping with stress successfully.

1. See something good in the stress. Families who cope well are able to find something positive in the stress and crises they face. For example, a family in which the father became ill and unable to work was thankful that he was home more and could spend time with his children.

2. Pull together. Members of healthy families unite when problems occur. No individual feels as though he must face his problems alone. Family members support and help one another.

3. Call on others for help. In addition to relying on immediate family members, members of healthy families turn to other resources for help. They seek out support from their church or synagogue, friends, neighbors, and extended family. Family friends may help with childcare or meals during illness. A church group may take up a special collection. An important resource is the family's ability to talk about the problem with each other.

4. Spiritual resources. Most families have spiritual convictions that help them cope with crises. Such convictions can be a source of stability to families who rely on them for their philosophy of life, perspective, and hope and comfort.

5. Keep communicating. Another resource that members of healthy families have is their ability to talk with each other during a crisis. For example, if one family member is struggling with grief or guilt over a mistake or a loss, the other family members are able to talk with them and help.

6. Go with the flow. Finally, strong families have learned that sometimes it is necessary just to stop fighting a problem and adapt to it. That may mean changing jobs, redefining who does what around the house, or cutting back on expenses. Even positive things like retirement, a wedding, or the birth of a child require the family to be adaptable and flexible. Being able to make necessary changes in family structure and traditions enables families to solve problems and retain close relationships. [77]

Successful families find a happy balance between stability and adaptability. For example, if Mom returns to work, some responsibilities, such as household chores, need to be redistributed. Retaining other things, like reading bedtime stories or playing board games, can maintain stability.

We usually think of stress as something to be avoided. That is not possible, nor is it necessarily desirable. While stress that reaches unmanageable levels is destructive, some stress is good. It motivates us to do more, keeps life interesting, and forces us to keep growing and learning.

A few additional thoughts on how to cope with stress:

- Take things one step, one day at a time.
- Stop worrying about things you cannot control.
- Do not let little things diminish your happiness. Clear them up or forget them.
- If possible, change your routine. Get variety in your life.
- Take time for a favorite activity.
- Meditate; pray.
- Learn to relax and take a fresh look at the problem.
- Get outside.
- Exercise.
- Learn to say no; cut back on demands and commitments.[78]

Lesson Sixteen
Problem Solving

Every world problem may be solved by obedience to the principles of the gospel of Jesus Christ.

—President David O. McKay[79]

FOLLOW-UP

(As a family, discuss the assignment for the lesson "Problem Prevention.")

1. What are some things we're doing to prevent problems in our family?
2. What more can we do to prevent possible problems?

CONCEPT

Every family has problems. How we handle our problems makes all the difference. These are some ideas on how to solve problems:

1. Focus on the present and be positive. Look toward a solution by asking, "How can we solve this problem?" instead of asking, "Why did this happen to us?" Try to see problems as challenges that you can overcome and as possible opportunities to learn and grow.

2. Keep the channels of communication open. Expressing feelings is an important part of surviving a crisis. All family members need to know they are heard and that their concerns are considered.

3. Seek solutions in small steps. Most problems don't have an easy fix. Tackle problems one step at a time.

4. Draw on spiritual resources. Heavenly Father will sustain and strengthen families in time of need when they turn to Him. Elder Paul H. Dunn said, "The Lord is waiting to help you cope today if you will lay your human-size needs at his divine feet" (*Ensign,* May 1979, 9).

Elder Boyd K. Packer gave individuals and families wise

counsel when he said, "When you have a problem, work it out in your own mind first. Ponder on it and analyze it and meditate on it. Read the scriptures. . . . Measure the problem against what you know to be right and wrong, and then make the decision. Then ask [the Lord] if the decision is right or if it is wrong" (*Ensign,* Aug. 1975, 88–89).

It will help families solve problems to develop "We can do it together" attitudes. Most problems can be solved when families talk about a problem as soon as it arises, discuss all possible solutions, then decide how they will "tackle it" together. Even huge conflicts can be resolved more easily when several people work together to find solutions.

Helping, supporting, and encouraging one another are keys to problem solving. Working through problems together strengthens relationships and helps bond family members to one another.

Elder Horacio A. Tenorio stated, "Problems form an important part of our lives. They are placed in our path for us to overcome them, not to be overcome by them. We must master them, not let them master us. Every time we overcome a challenge, we grow in experience, in self-assuredness, and in faith" (*Ensign,* May 1990, 79).

FAMILY SURVEY REVIEW
Statement 16: We can talk about things without arguing.

- Why is it important to be able to talk about things without arguing?
- What are some things we can do to keep from arguing?

STORY

The Brooklyn Bridge that spans the river between Manhattan and Brooklyn is simply an engineering miracle. In 1883, a creative engineer, John Roebling, was inspired by an idea for this spectacular bridge project. However, bridge-building experts told him to forget it—it just was not possible. Roebling convinced his son, Washington, an up-and-coming engineer, that the bridge could be built. The two of them conceived the concept of how it could be accomplished and how to overcome the obstacles. Somehow they convinced bankers to finance the project. Now, with unharnessed excitement and energy, they hired their crew and began to build their dream bridge.

The project was only a few months under way when a tragic on-site accident killed John Roebling and severely injured his son. Washington was severely brain damaged, unable to talk or walk. Everyone thought that the project would have to be scrapped since the Roeblings were the only ones who understood how the bridge could be built.

Though Washington Roebling was unable to move or talk, his mind was as sharp as ever. One day, as he lay in his hospital bed, an idea flashed into his mind as to how to develop a communication code. All he could move was one finger, so he touched the arm of his wife with that finger. In time she understood, and eventually he tapped out the code communicating what she was to tell the engineers who continued building the bridge. For thirteen years, Washington tapped out his instructions with one finger until the spectacular Brooklyn Bridge was finally completed.

—Contributed by Brian Cavanaugh[80]

DISCUSSION

1. Did Washington Roebling have a big problem?
2. Does every person and every family have problems?
3. What can we do as a family to improve our problem-solving skills?

ACTIVITY

First, let's talk about one problem that our family has. Let's decide today how we can work together to solve this problem. Second, let's do the activity called Family Contracts.

ASSIGNMENT

1. Make a greater effort to be aware of one another's problems. Try to raise your level of sensitivity to better recognize the challenges in other people's lives.
2. Ask for help with problems when you need it. Remember that to receive help with your problems, you need to share your concerns and challenges with those who care about you. There are always people who are willing to share your burdens.
3. Reach out to help others when they need you. As a family, look around to those in need. You can help solve others' problems by giving of yourselves in service. Who is someone your family can help? What can you do to help them?

ACTIVITY

FAMILY CONTRACTS

Creativity can often solve conflicts between family members. Those involved must be willing to talk about the problem, decide what needs to be done about it, and agree to try new ways of acting toward one another. Sometimes it helps to see the problem and proposed solution in writing. Written contracts can help family members work together on agreeable solutions for everyone.

ACTIVITY INSTRUCTIONS

1. The family members who have a problem need to choose a time to get together for a contract session.

2. Make sure everyone understands that the reason for getting together is not to argue or fight about the problem but to think about ways to solve it.

3. Use the steps of negotiation briefly outlined here to discuss the problem and possible solutions:

   • Be specific about defining the problem, and then brainstorm possible solutions.
   • Decide on a mutually agreeable solution.
   • Clearly define what each person agrees to do in order to make the solution work.
   • Discuss the consequences if anyone fails to comply.

4. Put the agreement in writing by using the contract on the following page, or design your own.

ACTIVITY

SAMPLE CONTRACT

Use the following example as a guide when making your own family contract. Encourage family members to be creative when putting their plan into words. Any format can be used as long as the contract is clear and understandable to everyone involved.

Whereas we,_____, and _____, hereby acknowledge that the following situation exists:_____
_____
_____
_____
_____
_____therefore in order to deal constructively with the above, we propose the following course of action: We, _____, and
_____, agree to
_____. In the event of noncompliance with the above terms, we agree to _____
_____
_____.

The following shall be an indication that the terms of this contract have been successfully completed: _____
_____
_____
_____.

In this event, we do solemnly agree to the following reward:_____
_____.

Date:_____

Signed:_____

Signed:_____

Solutions Through Stories and Poems: Choices

A Lesson Learned

I walked with my friend, a Quaker, to the newsstand the other night, and he bought a paper, thanking the newsie politely. The newsie didn't even acknowledge it.

"A sullen fellow, isn't he?" I commented.

"Oh, he's that way every night," shrugged my friend.

"Then why do you continue to be so polite to him?" I asked.

"Why not?" inquired my friend. "Why should I let *him* decide how I'm going to act?"

As I thought about this incident later, it occurred to me that the important word was "act." My friend *acts* toward people; most of us *react* toward them. His was a sense of inner balance which is lacking in most of us; he knows who he is, what he stands for, how he should behave. He refuses to return incivility for incivility, because then he would not be in command of his own conduct.

Nobody is unhappier than the perpetual reactor. His center of emotional gravity is not rooted within himself, where it belongs, but in the world outside him. His temperature is always being raised or lowered by the social climate around him, and he is a mere creature at the mercy of these elements.

Serenity cannot be achieved until we become the masters of our own actions and attitudes. To let another determine whether we shall be rude or gracious, elated or depressed, is to relinquish control over our own personalities, which is ultimately all we possess. The only true possession is self-possession.

—Contributed by Sydney J. Harris[81]

Obedience

More than a century ago the nobility of England, in their colorful finery, were on a fox hunt. They came to an area with a closed gate where a ragged youngster sat nearby.

"Open the gate, lad," said the leader of the hunt.

"No, this property belongs to my father, and he desires it left shut."

"Open the gate, lad. Do you know who I am?"

"No, sir."

"I am the Duke of Wellington."

"The Duke of Wellington, this nation's hero, would not ask me to disobey my father."

The riders of the hunt silently rode on.

—Author Unknown[82]

If

If you can keep your head when all about you
Are losing theirs and blaming it on you,
If you can trust yourself when all men doubt you,
But make allowance for their doubting too;
If you can wait and not be tired by waiting,
Or being lied about, don't deal in lies,
Or being hated, don't give way to hating,
And yet don't look too good, nor talk too wise;

If you can dream—and not make dreams your master;
If you can think—and not make thoughts your aim;
If you can meet with Triumph and Disaster
And treat those two imposters just the same;
If you can bear to hear the truth you've spoken
Twisted by knaves to make a trap for fools,
Or watch the things you gave your life to, broken,
And stoop and build 'em up with worn-out tools:

If you can make one heap of all your winnings
And risk it on one turn of pitch-and-toss,
And lose, and start again at your beginnings
And never breathe a word about your loss;
If you can force your heart and nerve and sinew
To serve your turn long after they are gone,
And so hold on when there is nothing in you
Except the Will which says to them: "Hold on!"

If you can talk with crowds and keep your virtue,
Or walk with Kings—nor lose the common touch,
If neither foes nor loving friends can hurt you,
If all men count with you, but none too much;
If you can fill the unforgiving minute
With sixty seconds' worth of distance run,
Yours is the Earth and everything that's in it,
And—which is more—you'll be a Man, my son!

—Rudyard Kipling[83]

IF I CAN STOP ONE HEART FROM BREAKING

If I can stop one Heart from breaking,
I shall not live in vain;
If I can ease one Life the Aching,
Or cool one pain,
Or help one fainting Robin
Unto his Nest again,
I shall not live in vain.

—Emily Dickinson[84]

AROUND THE CORNER

Around the corner I have a friend,
In this great city that has no end;
Yet, days go by and weeks rush on,
And before I know it a year has gone.
And I never see my old friend's face;
For life is a swift and terrible race.
He knows I like him just as well
As in the days when I rang his bell
And he rang mine.

We were younger then.
And now we are busy, tired men:
Tired with playing a foolish game;
Tired with trying to make a name;
"Tomorrow," I say, "I will call on Jim,
Just to show I'm thinking of him."
But tomorrow comes and tomorrow goes;
And the distance between us grows and grows.

Around the corner! Yet miles away . . .
"Here's a telegram, sir—'Jim died today.'"

And that's what we get—and deserve in the end—
Around the corner, a vanished friend.

—Charles Hanson Towne[85]

THE MAN WHO THINKS HE CAN

If you think you are beaten, you are;
If you think you dare not, you don't.
If you like to win but think you can't,
It's almost a cinch you won't. . . .
Life's battles don't always go
To the stronger or faster man;
But soon or late the man who wins
Is the man who thinks he can.

—Walter D. Wintle[86]

YOU

You are the person who has to decide
Whether you'll do it or toss it aside.
You are the fellow who makes up your mind
Whether you'll lead or will linger behind.
Whether you'll try for the goal that's afar
Or just be contented to stay where you are.

What do you wish? To be known as a shirk,
Known as a good man who's willing to work,
Scorned as a loafer, or praised by your chief
Rich man or poor man or beggar or thief?
Eager or earnest or dull through the day?
Honest or crooked? It's you who must say!
You must decide in the face of the test
Whether you'll shirk or give it your best.

Nobody here will compel you to rise;
No one will force you to open your eyes;
No one will answer for you, yes or no,
Whether to stay or whether you go;
Life is a game, but it's you who must say
Whether as cheat or as sportsman you'll play.
Fate may betray you, but you settle first
Whether to live to your best or your worst.

So whatever it is you are wanting to be
Remember, to fashion the choice you are free.
Kindly or selfish, or gentle or strong,
Keeping the right way or taking the wrong,
Careless of honor or guarding your pride,
All these are questions which you must decide.
Yours the selection, whichever you do;
The thing men call character's all up to you.

—Edgar A. Guest[87]

Chapter Five
Well-Being Solution

Cease to be idle; cease to be unclean; cease to find fault one with another; cease to sleep longer than is needful; retire to thy bed early, that ye may not be weary; arise early, that your bodies and your minds may be invigorated.

—Doctrine and Covenants 88:124

Introduction for Parents

A businessman in Texas shared what he learned about well-being when he told this true story:

I started my adult life with a bang, you might say. My parents were moderately well-to-do and gave me a good start in my own business. It flourished and things looked rosy for ten years or so. Then the economy went sour at about the time I had made some risky investments. One by one those went down the tubes. In the end we lost everything—house, cars, and the business.

My wife and I sat out by the lake one night and talked until the sun came up. I remember feeling like I had been stripped of everything—like I had been robbed. "Why try again?" I asked her. "We may work and work only to lose it." We struggled with that a long time. Finally, we decided that we had been thinking wrong. The purpose of life isn't to accumulate money, swimming pools, cars, and fur coats. The purpose of life is to enjoy life because it is a precious gift—to cherish your family and friends, to become a better person intellectually and spiritually, and to help other people. The investments of time and effort I make in family and friends, in charitable work, and in improving myself can never be lost. Things in the mind and heart cannot be taken away.

We did start over again and have enjoyed success. We've replaced many of the material things we lost, but most importantly, we have changed our thoughts. The job, the possessions, the money are no longer an end in themselves. They are a means of making life pleasant and serving others. If I lost them all tomorrow, I would still feel rich.[88]

Total well-being is an ideal state when a balance is achieved in the six areas of life: physical, mental, social, emotional, financial, and spiritual. Realistically, however, seldom do individuals or families enjoy well-being in every area at the same time. For example, even though we may enjoy total physical well-being, if we are stressed financially, we don't have peace of mind. The reverse can also be true. If we have financial independence, but we are burdened with serious ill health, we don't enjoy total well-being. Achieving a balance in all areas is a process and a goal.

The wisest course individuals and families can follow is to make the kind of choices that will ensure well-being in as many areas as possible.

FAMILIES WHO ENJOY WELL-BEING:

1. *Strive to live righteous lives and work individually and together to inherit exaltation in the celestial kingdom.* As these families keep the commandments and follow the prophet and Church leaders, they can enjoy the companionship of the Holy Ghost. The Lord has promised that when we are doing all we possibly can to obey and draw near unto Him, then He will draw near unto us. I believe that the Lord's presence ensures well-being.

2. *Demonstrate love and respect for one another.* Where love is, harmony exists. Parents and children, make sincere and continued efforts to love one another unselfishly and preserve peace in the home.

3. *Have a positive outlook on life and a sense of humor.* Positive attitudes are contagious. In families we have incredible power to affect one another with our attitudes—in positive and negative ways. A saying that I heard once was posted on our refrigerator for years: "Be wise if you can, be pretty if you are, but be cheerful if it kills you!" Optimism and a sense of humor are virtues every family needs in large quantities.

4. *Help one another live correct values and reach worthy goals.* There truly is strength in numbers. Families who enjoy well-being meet together and set rules and goals, then they help one another obey the rules and achieve the goals. We can feel the unity and righteous power of our family when we're working together to reach exaltation.

5. *Work toward reaching individual potentials within a caring, supportive environment.* What a difference it makes when our family supports us in our interests and activities! We're usually happier and more successful when our family is there for us when we need them.

6. *Build strong relationships with one another.* People aren't best friends just because they were born into the same family. Strong relationships require time and effort. Usually good relationships result from years of speaking and acting in ways that demonstrate concern and affection. Family members have countless opportunities to build strong, long-lasting relationships. That's one of the blessings of being a family.

7. *Live a healthy lifestyle.* When we're free from illness and pain we can more easily work on reaching our mental, social, emotional, financial, and spiritual goals. Health is a gift we should work daily to protect.

8. *Encourage the mental development of each family member.* Strong families help one another with school and work assignments, read books, share uplifting music, and encourage intellectual growth.

9. *Promote and teach social skills.* Through example and precept parents can teach social skills that will benefit children throughout their lives.

10. *Serve others gladly.* When we unselfishly serve our fellowmen with no thought of reward or recognition, we are blessed. Helping others always contributes to our own well-being.

11. *Attain an emotional balance.* Families who enjoy well-being discuss problems before they get out of control. They have learned that extreme reactions are not productive.

12. *Achieve financial stability.* Healthy families recognize the difference between a need and a want. They live in such a way that money doesn't become a source of conflict.

13. *Recognize problems and conflicts, but focus on dealing with the problems and growing from the challenges.* With most family problems the entire family should gather together, discuss the problem, and consider possible solutions. After every family member has shared his or her opinion, a solution is chosen and the family works together to solve the problem. During family discussions and after problems are past the crisis stage, ask questions like, "How can we learn from this?" or "What can we do to prevent this from happening again?" Strong families learn and grow closer from their challenges.

14. *Adapt to change well.* Change is an inevitable part of life. Those who enjoy well-being have learned to view this life through a "wide-angle lens," with a long-term perspective that understands the necessity of change. They take advantage of the growth change offers.

15. *Learn from the past, live in the present, and look to the future.* Healthy families don't live in the past or the future. From the past they take the best and discard the rest. In the present they enjoy every minute and work hard so their future will be bright. They look toward the future with hope of attaining their righteous desires.

It is apparent that there are serious problems in this world. Many people stand in need of help. However, it is also true that there is much happiness and well-being in the world. When individuals enjoy well-being and are members of strong families, those individuals can encourage well-being in others and can contribute to the success of communities and nations.

Just as individuals grow and develop one day at a time, family well-being is also a process. Creating things of great worth always takes considerable time and effort. We need to be kind and patient with ourselves and with our families as we strive to achieve well-being.

Lesson Seventeen
Physical Well-Being

Your physical well-being is not only a priceless blessing to yourself, but a heritage that you may pass on to your descendants. With good health, all other activities of life are greatly enhanced.
—President Ezra Taft Benson (*New Era*, Sep. 1979, 42)

FOLLOW-UP

(As a family, discuss the assignment for the lesson "Problem Solving.")

1. What did we learn from the lesson on problem solving?
2. How have we improved our problem-solving skills?

CONCEPT

Prophets through the ages have taught us the importance of keeping our bodies healthy and strong. We can usually be more effective in other areas of our lives (mental, social, physical, and spiritual) if we maintain our health. Most families who have a healthy lifestyle live the Word of Wisdom (D&C 89). They also try to:

1. Drink plenty of clean water.
2. Eat well-balanced meals, including fruits, vegetables, and whole grains.
3. Exercise regularly.
4. Get adequate sleep.

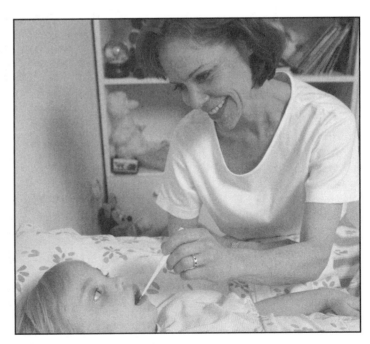

Being healthy affects the quality of our lives. Having a strong body gives us the energy and ability to do our daily activities, and our outlook on life is usually better. When our physical needs have been met, we can better reach out to meet the needs of others.

How blessed we are to have been given special instructions from the Lord about how to keep our bodies strong and healthy—the Word of Wisdom.

President Joseph F. Smith counseled us when he said, "Now I do wish with all my heart—not because I say it, but because it is written in the word of the Lord—that you would give heed to [the] Word of Wisdom. It was given to us . . . for our guidance, for our happiness and advancement in every principle that pertains to the kingdom of God, in time and throughout eternity, and I pray you to observe it. It will do you good; it will ennoble your souls; it will free your thoughts and your hearts from the spirit of destruction; . . . it will bring you nearer to the similitude of the Son of God, the Savior of the world."[89]

President Gordon B. Hinckley remarked, "Look upon the Word of Wisdom as more than a commonplace thing. I regard it as the most remarkable document on health of which I know. It came to the Prophet Joseph Smith in 1833, when relatively little was known of dietary matters. Now the greater the scientific research, the more certain becomes the proof of Word of Wisdom principles. The evidence against tobacco is now overwhelming . . . the evidence against liquor is just as great" (*Ensign,* May 1998, 49–50).

The Apostle Paul asked, "Know ye not that ye are the temple of God and that the Spirit of God dwelleth in you? . . . the temple of God is holy, which temple ye are" (1 Cor. 3:16–17). May we each conscientiously care for our earthly tabernacles . . . the bodies given us from our loving Heavenly Father.

FAMILY SURVEY REVIEW
Statement 17: Our family has good health habits.

- Why is it important to keep ourselves healthy and physically fit?
- How are we doing with our health habits? Do we eat healthfully? Do we exercise regularly?
- How can we improve?

STORY

This story was told by Elder N. Eldon Tanner:

I should like to tell you the experience of one of our young men, [whom] we will call John, who went east to an officers' training school. A new commanding officer came into the school, and they put on a banquet to honor him. There, by every plate, was a cocktail glass. When the proper time came, every one of those potential officers stood up with his cocktail glass to toast that incoming officer—that is, all but one boy, and he raised a glass of milk. It would take a lot of courage, wouldn't it, to stand there with all those officers and see all of those cocktail glasses come up, and stand and raise a glass of milk!

Well, the officer saw it, and he made a beeline for that boy after the entertainment was over and said, "Why did you toast me with a glass of milk?"

"Well, sir," he said, "I've never touched alcohol in my life. I don't want to touch it; my parents wouldn't want me to touch it; and I didn't think you would want me to either. I wanted to toast you, so I thought you would be satisfied if I toasted you with what I am accustomed to drinking."

The officer said, "Report to my headquarters in the morning."

I suppose that boy spent a sleepless night, but when he went to the officer's quarters the next morning, do you know what happened? The officer assigned him a place on his staff with this explanation: "I want to surround myself with men who have the courage to do what they think is right regardless of what anybody else thinks about it" (*Ensign,* May 1976, 43–44).

DISCUSSION

1. What did John toast the officer with?
2. What did the officer think about John?
3. What do you suppose that your friends think about you when you live the gospel?

ACTIVITY

Improve your physical well-being by doing something active as a family. Go on a walk, swim, play ball, or choose another activity. Make sure to include everyone.

Ask, "Can we go on a family walk right now?" If not now, ask, "When can we do something active as a family?"

ASSIGNMENT

The assignment is to make a specific plan of how your family will improve its physical well-being. Then the challenge is to do it.

PHYSICAL WELL-BEING ACTIVITY IDEAS

- Go on a walk.
- Ride a bike.
- Swim.
- Go hiking.
- Exercise while you watch TV.
- Play tag.
- Lift weights.
- Play Frisbee in the park.
- Play ball—soccer, kickball, basketball, softball.
- Skate or roller blade.

Lesson Eighteen

Mental Well-Being

*Put forth your ability to learn as fast as you can, and gather all
the strength of mind and principle of faith you possibly can, and
then distribute your knowledge to the people.*

—Brigham Young[90]

FOLLOW-UP

(As a family, discuss the assignment for the lesson "Physical Well-Being.")

1. What improvements have we made in our eating and exercising habits?
2. Did we make a plan of how we'll improve our physical well-being? If not, let's decide on some ways we can do this. (Ideas are in the Physical Well-Being Lesson.)
3. If we have a plan for improvement, what are we doing to follow it?

CONCEPT

People with good mental well-being have an optimistic outlook on life and enjoy learning. They want to know about many subjects and welcome new information that will help them understand themselves, other people, and the world.

President Gordon B. Hinckley counseled us, "Get all the education you can . . . Cultivate skills of mind and hands. Education is the key to opportunity."[91]

One ideal way to improve our minds is to read. Through books we are taught important lessons from history; we can visit any place in the world and become experts on many subjects.

Another good place to learn is at the dinner table. When families are all together, they can talk about what they learned that day. Parents can tell about interesting things that happened at work or discuss local and national news. Children can share the events of their day at school and play.

Instead of watching television, families can choose to enjoy activities that will improve their lives and strengthen their relationships. A list, "Things to Do instead of Watching TV, Playing Video Games, or Surfing the Internet" is included in this lesson. Sheryl Kempton remarked, "While there are some wonderful programs on television that offer education, wholesome entertainment, or both, we need to learn to be selective. It is seldom true that there is *nothing* better to do than watching television. If television is frequently our first choice, we may be losing either our creativity or our desire to serve. Perhaps we could try to cultivate them a little more by spending less time sitting in front of the television being passively entertained and spending more time actively developing our talents and serving others" (*Ensign,* Aug. 1986, 56). This same counsel applies also to movies, video games, and the Internet.

Besides changing some of our everyday activities, attitude is an important part of mental well-being. The well-known artist known as Whistler had ideas about how we can enjoy mental well-being. Whistler said, "Hang on the walls of your mind the memory of your successes. Take counsel of your strength, not your weakness. Think of the good jobs you have done. Think of the times when you rose above your average level of performance and carried out an idea or a dream or a desire for which you had deeply longed. Hang these pictures on the walls of your mind and look at them as you travel the roadway of life" (quoted by Elder Sterling W. Still, in *Ensign,* June 1971, 44).

We will be contributing to our mental well-being when we think good thoughts about ourselves, our circumstances, our family, our neighbors, and all we meet. Happiness is not a destination; it is a state of mind.

Elder M. Russell Ballard taught, "Attitude is an important part of the foundation upon which we build a productive life. In appraising our present attitude, we might ask: 'Am I working to become my best self? Do I set worthy and attainable goals? Do I look toward the positive in life? Am I alert to ways that I can render more and better service? Am I doing more than is required of me?' Remember, a good attitude produces good results, a fair attitude fair results, a poor attitude poor results. We each shape our own life, and the shape of it is determined largely by our attitude" (*Ensign,* May 1981, 86).

FAMILY SURVEY REVIEW
Statement 18: We enjoy learning in our family.

- What are some of the ways people learn that our family would enjoy?
- How do you feel about sharing at the dinner table one thing you learned each day?

STORY

A man was complaining to a friend about his trials and difficulties. After a while the complaining became too much for the friend. "I see you have been living on Grumbling Street. I lived there myself for some time and never enjoyed good health. The air was bad, the house bad, the water bad; the birds never came and sang in the streets, and I was quite gloomy and sad. But I moved. I found myself a house on Thanksgiving Street, and ever since, I have had good health, and so has my family. The air is pure, the water pure, the house good. The sun shines on it all day, and I am as happy as I can be. Now I recommend that you move too. There are plenty of houses available on Thanksgiving Street, and I'm sure you'd find yourself to be a new man. I would be glad to have you as a neighbor!"[92]

DISCUSSION

   1. What does it mean to live on Grumbling Street?

   2. Has our family ever lived on Grumbling Street? When?

   3. What does it mean to live on Thanksgiving Street? Shall we move there? When?

ACTIVITY

For the activity, parents are to lead the following discussion:

Elder James E. Faust remarked, "One of the main problems in families today is that we spend less and less time together. Some spend an extraordinary amount of time, when they are together, in front of the television, which robs them of personal time for reinforcing feelings of self-worth. Time together is precious time—time needed to talk, to listen, to encourage, and to show [each other] how to do things" (*Ensign,* May 1983, 41).

Often television programs, movies, and video games teach children things they shouldn't learn. Parents wouldn't think of letting someone come into their home and teach children to be disrespectful to adults, exhibit low moral values, and enjoy violence. Yet that is what happens when children are allowed to watch excessive, unmonitored television, movies, and video games. Educational and uplifting programs and movies are available, and families can share special times watching together. The media can be used as a tool for learning good things, but families need to be discerning and careful.

Let's talk about our family's habits of media entertainment. Do we have a problem? How do we all feel about how we spend our free time? Below is a list of things to do instead of watching TV, playing video games, or surfing the Internet. If our family has a problem in this area, let's decide on some limits. Then let's choose activities from the list below and schedule time to do them.

Breaking bad habits is difficult, but not impossible. It will bring rewards of closer family relationships and increased mental well-being. The best way to break bad habits is to replace them with good habits.

Things to Do Instead of Watching TV, Playing Video Games, or Surfing the Internet:

- Do a kind deed for someone.
- Practice a musical instrument.
- Help with the housework or the yard work.
- Work on a hobby or begin a new hobby.
- Visit someone who is sick or shut in.
- Read.
- Exercise.
- Write a letter.
- Play a sport.
- Invite a friend to visit.
- Finish an unfinished project.
- Cook.
- Play a board or card game.

- Listen to music.
- Go to a movie, play, or concert.
- Put together a puzzle.
- Go on a hike or picnic.
- Go swimming.

ASSIGNMENT

The assignment for this lesson is to do one of the things listed below to increase your mental well-being:

1. Take a trip to the library.
2. Enjoy an evening reading as a family with all the "electronics" turned off.
3. Assign family members to bring one item of educational interest or information about a current event to discuss at the dinner table.
4. Give a lesson that teaches a moral value.
5. As a family, discuss what to do in case of a fire or other emergency.

If time and interest allow, do the Additional Activity: Family Yearbook on the following page. Or read the Additional Solution for Success: Family Esteem.

ADDITIONAL ACTIVITY
FAMILY YEARBOOK

Now and then it's enjoyable to reflect on important, often life-changing family events of the past. This activity can help you look back and recall past times, discuss the important things that have happened in your family, and renew a long-term perspective and appreciation for one another.

ACTIVITY INSTRUCTIONS

1. At the end of the year, gather together all the photos taken of your family that year.

2. Choose the photos that best show favorite past events.

3. Decide how to organize the photos. You may want to use them:

    - In the order they were taken
    - In sections for each member of the family
    - In sections according to themes (trips, school, etc.)

4. Secure the pictures in a safe, archival format and write captions.

5. Include other mementos, such as postcards, invitations, or announcements, if you like.

6. Have pages at the back of your yearbook for everyone to write their name and comments about the year.

ADDITIONAL SOLUTION FOR SUCCESS

FAMILY ESTEEM

Just as individuals need to feel good about themselves in order to be successful, families need to have a feeling of worth and value about themselves as a group. They need to be able to look to the future with confidence that they can be successful.

Families can learn to believe in themselves and their ability to solve problems and be happy. This belief begins with an understanding that each family is unique with its own special talents and strengths.

In all the world there isn't another family exactly like yours. There isn't any other family made up of exactly the same people, with the same combination of talents, skills, challenges, etc. No other family has had just the same experiences, felt the same joys, or experienced quite the same disappointments. Your family has its own terms for certain things, nicknames for each other, special stories, and jokes. Of all the families that have ever been formed, or that will be formed, there has never been, or ever will be, another one exactly like yours.

In addition to appreciating their worth together, strong families value each individual family member. They know that each person contributes something to the family that no one else can. The family's belief in each one of its members creates a great sense of self-worth and security for each individual. In turn, the self-esteem of each individual contributes to the whole family's sense of worth.

For those who value their family, how they see themselves is more important than what others think of them. Believing in and accepting who we are is one of the most difficult challenges in life. We are constantly bombarded with messages like, "What makes you think you can do it?" "Kids your size can't be on the team." "You're too fat to be a cheerleader." "Why doesn't your family get a decent car?" We must have a personal awareness of our worth regardless of how other people judge us. If we can believe in ourselves, the self-defeating messages of who we ought to be, or what we ought to be, cannot damage our sense of worth.

When the great scientist Albert Einstein was ten years old, he was told by his school teacher, "You will never amount to much." Einstein later wrote, "Try not to become a man of success but rather try to become a man of value."[93] He was able to be himself, ignoring the false opinion of others. What other people think of us isn't important unless we let it be. When family members are determined to believe in each other, it is easier for each family member to believe in himself or herself, too.

The poet E. E. Cummings recognized the same challenges when he wrote, "To be nobody but yourself in a world which is doing its best, night and day, to make you everybody else, means to fight the hardest battle which any human being can fight; and never stop fighting."[94] In reality, to base our sense of worth on what others think of us is to be more responsible to them than we are to ourselves. Let's not allow our family's self-esteem to be determined by outside influences.

Social Well-Being

You can be excellent in every way. You can be first class. There is no need for you to be a scrub. Respect yourself. Do not feel sorry for yourself. Do not dwell on unkind things others may say about you. . . . Polish and refine whatever talents the Lord has given you. Go forward in life with a twinkle in your eye and a smile on your face, but with great and strong purpose in your heart. Love life and look for its opportunities, and forever and always be loyal to the Church.

—President Gordon B. Hinckley (*Ensign*, May 2001, 95)

FOLLOW-UP

(As a family, discuss the assignment for the lesson "Mental Well-Being.")

1. What are some of the things we've learned that improve our mental well-being?
2. Are our dinner conversations more enjoyable? If not, what can we do to improve?

CONCEPT

One of the roads to happiness is social well-being. When we are socially involved with others, we're usually happier and feel a part of a larger group. Supportive friends, extended family, and neighbors can give us help and encouragement when needed. We all like to know that people care about us. More importantly, our families should always be involved in quiet acts of selfless service as we reach out to others.

Elder Marvin J. Ashton said, "We . . . tend to evaluate others on the basis of physical, outward appearance: their 'good looks,' their social status, their family pedigrees, their degrees, or their economic situations. The Lord, however, has a different standard by which he measures a person. . . . When the Lord measures an individual, He does not take a tape measure around the person's head to determine his mental capacity, nor his chest to determine his manliness, but He measures the heart as an indictor of the person's capacity and potential to bless others" (*Ensign,* Nov. 1988, 15).

What is social well-being? It is:
- Feeling accepted in a group
- Helping others feel appreciated and accepted
- Spending quality time with others
- Communicating openly and listening well
- Helping people deal with conflict and crises in constructive ways
- Committing time and energy to causes that benefit others

President Joseph F. Smith stated, "Our children should be taught to respect not only their fathers and their mothers, and their brothers and sisters, but they should be taught to respect all mankind, and especially should they be instructed and taught and brought up to honor the aged and the infirm, the unfortunate and the poor, the needy, and those who need the sympathies of mankind" (*Conference Report,* Oct. 1904, 87).

To enjoy social well-being in our families, we need to interact with other people, be involved with those who can help and strengthen us when needed, and reach beyond our own concerns to be part of a support system for others. As we share our lives, we'll experience the joys of social well-being.

FAMILY SURVEY REVIEW
Statement 19: Our family enjoys being with other people.

- How can our family be more friendly and social?
- What can we do to be of service to our extended family and to our friends?

STORY

Sam Foss liked to walk. He had wandered a bit too far today in the blazing sun, lost in his thoughts; and now suddenly he realized how hot and tired he was. The big tree at the side of the road looked tempting, and he stopped for a moment to rest in its shade.

There was a little sign on the tree, and he read it with surprise and pleasure. "There is a good spring inside the fence. Come and drink if you are thirsty."

Foss climbed over the fence, found the spring, and gratefully drank his fill of the cool water. Then he noticed a bench near the spring, and tacked to the bench another sign. He went over to it and read, "Sit down and rest awhile if you are tired."

Now thoroughly delighted, he went to a barrel of apples nearby—and saw that here, too, was a sign! "If you like apples, just help yourself," he read. He accepted the invitation, picked out a plump red apple, and looked up to discover an elderly man watching him with interest.

"Hello, there!" he called. "Is this your place?"

"Yes," the old man answered. "I'm glad you stopped by." [Then the man] explained the reason for the signs. The water was going to waste; the bench was gathering dust in the attic; the apples were more than they could use. He and his wife thought it would be neighborly to offer tired, thirsty passers-by a place to rest and refresh themselves. So they had brought down the bench and put up the signs—and made themselves a host of fine new friends!

"You must like people," Foss said.

"Of course," the old man answered simply. "Don't you?"

—Contibuted by Sam Walter Foss[95]

DISCUSSION

1. Did the sharing man help make other people happy?
2. Can we share something we have to make another family happy? What?
3. Is life more enjoyable with friends? How can we be better friends?

ACTIVITY

The activity for this lesson is to do something as a family that will improve our social well-being. Here are some ideas:

- Meet all of our neighbors.
- Volunteer our time in service to the community.
- Visit a nursing home or hospital.
- Invite friends to dinner or to play games with our family.
- Do something kind for a neighbor.
- Call a friend or relative we haven't spoken to for a long time.

ASSIGNMENT

The assignment is to make a specific plan of how your family will improve its long-term social well-being. Then the challenge is to do it. Some additional ideas can be found in the Additional Activity: Family Fun, and the Additional Activity: Being Part of an Extended Family.

ADDITIONAL ACTIVITY
FAMILY FUN

Most families agree that it's important to spend quality time together having fun. However, busy lives often prevent family members from doing it. This activity is designed to help us make definite plans that include our entire family, and to turn those plans into reality.

1. Take a sheet of paper and fold it in half. On one side, we'll write our ideas for things our family can do together at no cost (playing games, taking a hike, etc.). On the other side, we'll write ideas for things our family can do that cost money (movies, dinner in a restaurant, vacations, etc.).

2. Read all of the ideas and cross out activities that we're not really interested in.

3. Talk about all of the activities that don't cost money. Next, we'll copy the good suggestions onto small slips of paper, put them into a jar or box, and label it "Free Fun."

4. Discuss the ideas that do cost money. We'll put the list of those activities into a jar or box we label "Fun Funds." Now let's decide how our family can save money to put in the box. Here are some ideas to consider:
   • Everyone "pledges" an amount from paychecks or allowances each week.
   • Everyone agrees to give ten percent of all gift money received for birthdays, holidays, and special occasions.
   • At the end of each day, everyone tosses in all of their loose change.
   • All loose change left in pockets from the laundry goes in the box.
   • Family members can donate the money received from recycling aluminum cans or another fund-raising project.
   • Parents might agree to "match" whatever amount has been saved during a time period.

5. Schedule at least one time each week for our family to do something together from the "Free Fun" box.

6. Decide what our family wants to do first from the "FUN FUNDS" box. As soon as there is enough money, we'll schedule a time for the activity and start saving for the next one on the list.

7. When our family has used all the ideas in the boxes, we can start over again.

ADDITIONAL ACTIVITY

BEING PART OF AN EXTENDED FAMILY

A sense of belonging and increased social well-being comes from being part of an extended family. This includes feeling a part of our family's history and knowing the stories about our grandpa and grandma, and the way life was for our ancestors. It also involves an interest and concern for the younger members of the extended family.

People with a strong sense of family pass on the stories of deceased family members so that younger members can learn about their roots. Alex Haley, author of the book *Roots,* tells about the outpouring of interest American families had in the history he uncovered regarding African-Americans. Mr. Haley believes that many people feel a little empty because they don't know about their ancestors.[96] Preserving and passing on family history is important for a family's sense of continuity. The feeling a family has about who they are, because of an ancestor's example of how they coped with adversities, can be a source of strength. Looking at our ancestors' lives and history can also help us put our problems in perspective. The struggles they endured and the joys they felt give us a better understanding of ourselves.

In addition to learning from their family history, families can also learn much from their living relatives. Grandparents and other relatives who give their time and love to children strengthen their families. Relatives can tell the children what their parents were like as children. From their experience, they can teach and share valuable advice. Quite often grandparents are the nucleus of extended family activities.

An appreciation for the past also demonstrates to older relatives a respect for their values and accomplishments. The life of grandparents can be given renewed meaning by a grandchild's interest.

Strong families keep in touch with their extended family. They pass news back and forth, exchange pictures, or call each other for no particular reason. Families who live far apart may do things such as circulate a letter to which each family adds his or her own news before mailing it on. They may make tape-recordings for family members far away. Some families devote a whole wall to pictures of grandparents, aunts, uncles, and cousins. The key is having enough contact with each other so that relatives feel like relatives, not strangers.

To strengthen your family's ties to your extended family, conduct a little quiz about your relatives. Add as many questions as you would like.

For Children:

- Who is our oldest relative?
- Who is our youngest relative?
- How many cousins do we have?
- How are we related to all our aunts and uncles?
- Where did our ancestors come from? Where did they live? What were their names? What did they do?
- Where were our grandparents (or other relatives) born?
- How old are they?
- What did they do for a living?

For Parents:

- What do you remember most about your grandparents as a little child? as a teenager? as an adult?
- What other relative was a favorite of yours? Why?
- What things did you do with relatives when you were growing up?

For Everyone:

- What is the importance of our extended family?
- What things do we not know about our family's history that we would like to know?
- Are there relatives with whom we would like to spend more time?
- What can we do to strengthen our extended family relationships?

Lesson Twenty

Financial Well-Being

Our inspired leaders have always urged us to get out of debt, live within our means, and pay as we go.

—President Ezra Taft Benson (*Ensign,* June 1987, 3)

FOLLOW-UP

(As a family, discuss the assignment for the lesson "Social Well-Being.")

1. What are we doing to know our neighbors and extended family members better?
2. What acts of kindness and service have we performed since our last lesson?

CONCEPT

Ideally, families should live in such a way that money doesn't become a source of conflict. Usually our financial problems aren't money problems; they're attitude and behavior problems.

President N. Eldon Tanner remarked, "I am convinced that it is not the amount of money an individual earns that brings peace of mind as much as it is having control of his money. . . . Those who structure their standard of living to allow a little surplus control their circumstances. Those who spend a little more than they earn are controlled by their circumstances" (*Ensign,* June 1982, 4).

What are some things we can do to meet our needs and reach our financial goals? We can:

- **Pay an honest tithe.** "Bring ye all the tithes into the storehouse . . . and prove me now herewith, saith the Lord of hosts, if I will not open you the windows of heaven and pour you out a blessing, that there shall not be room enough to receive it" (Mal. 3:10). David B. Haight counseled, "Pay your tithing

monthly or weekly as you are paid. Never be in debt to the Lord" (*Ensign,* May 1981, 42).

- **Learn.** Do our best to get a good education and continue learning.

- **Work diligently.** There is no substitute for simply working hard to get what we want in life.

- **Improve job skills.** Continue looking for educational and job opportunities that will qualify us for better employment or improve our life.

- **Plan.** Make a plan for how we'll spend our income.

- **Commit.** Commit to our financial plan. For example, we must realize that there will be times when we have to wait for something we want until there is money for it. Usually we can live without things we want but don't really need.

- **Live the plan.** There will sometimes be unexpected bills, but as a rule, we should live by a plan that will keep us as debt free as possible. If we really want to be out of debt, we should decide that there will be no more charging or borrowing money. Nothing will be purchased until there is enough money to pay for it.

- **Save for the future.** We should try to save some of our money each month for our future needs and for unexpected expenses (accidents, layoffs, etc.).

President Heber J. Grant taught, "If there is any one thing that will bring peace and contentment into the human heart, and into the family, it is to live within our means, and if there is any one thing that is grinding and discouraging and disheartening, it is to have debts and obligations that one cannot meet" (*Relief Society Magazine,* May 1932, 302).

When families make wise financial decisions and live within their means, they experience less stress and fewer problems, and they can enjoy financial well-being.

FAMILY SURVEY REVIEW
Statement 20: Our family makes wise financial decisions.

- What good decisions do we make with our money?
- How can we stay out of debt?
- What should we do to save money?

STORY

An old fable tells about an ant and a grasshopper. All summer long the ant busily worked, preparing for the cold winter ahead. The grasshopper watched the ant and laughed at her. "Stop working and come and play!" the grasshopper said. "Don't worry about winter. The sun is shining and we are young!" Nevertheless, the ant continued to put away food, preparing for the months ahead. The grasshopper kept playing.

Before too long, the snow fell and their world became a white, frozen land. The ant was snug and warm, with plenty of food in her little home. The grasshopper, you might guess, was miserably cold and hungry.

—Aesop's Fables[97]

DISCUSSION

1. What can we learn from the ant?
2. What do we learn from the grasshopper?
3. Is our family like the ant or the grasshopper? How?

ACTIVITY

Running our home costs money. We need a budget to help us stay out of debt. In the April 1999 General Conference, Elder Robert D. Hales remarked, "Teach our children by example how to budget time and resources. Help them learn self-reliance and the importance of preparing for the future" (*Ensign,* May 1999, 33). It's easier to live debt free when we understand how much money we have to work with and what our family expenses are. This activity can help us look at our monthly expenses and see where the money is spent. First, let's guess the answers to these questions:

1. What is the price of a gallon of milk?
2. What is the price of a loaf of bread?
3. What does our family spend each month on food?
4. How much does it cost to fill the car with gas?
5. What do we pay each month for rent (or the mortgage payment)?
6. What was last month's telephone bill?
7. How much did we pay last month for gas and electricity?
8. How much does it cost to have the dentist fill a cavity?
9. What does it cost to replace a light bulb?
10. How much does it cost to go to college?

Let's play the "Money Game." In preparation for this game, a parent will need to have real or pretend money in the amount of your monthly paycheck or the amount you use for paying bills. On the table, display all the money.

Explain: "The first thing we do is take out ten percent for tithing." (Take that amount away and put it in an envelope.)

Ask: "Family, how much of this money does it take to pay the rent (mortgage) for one month?" (Take that amount away and put it in an envelope.)

Ask: "How much money does it take to buy the food for one month?" (Put that amount in an envelope.)

Ask: "How much money does it take to pay the utilities bill?" (Put that amount in an envelope. Do this until all of your bills are "paid.")

Ask: "Family, how much money does our family have left each month for extra purchases? How much money do we have to save? What should we do about this?"

ASSIGNMENT

1. Decide as a family on a budget. First, list all of your bills and expenses. Decide how much money you have to spend on your needs. Now talk about your wants and how much money you should spend on those. Last, discuss how much money your family should save each month and how you will do that.
2. For one week, each family member should keep a record of every purchase. Then meet again and discuss how well you're staying within your budget.
3. Each day try to make choices that will help you be debt free and save for the future.
4. Read the Additional Solution for Success: Ten Financial Principles on the following page.

ADDITIONAL SOLUTION FOR SUCCESS
TEN FINANCIAL PRINCIPLES

1. Financial problems are usually behavioral problems rather than money problems.

2. If you continue doing what you have been doing, you'll continue getting what you have been getting.

3. Nothing (no thing) is worth risking the loss of a relationship.

4. Money spent on things you value usually leads to a feeling of satisfaction and accomplishment. Money spent on things you don't value usually leads to a feeling of frustration and futility.

5. We know the price of everything and the value of nothing.

6. You can never get enough of what you don't need, because what you don't need can never satisfy you.

7. Financial freedom is more often the result of decreased spending than of increased income.

8. You should be grateful for what you have.

9. The best things in life are free.

10. The value of an individual should never be equated with the bank account of an individual.[98]

SOLUTIONS THROUGH STORIES AND POEMS: WELL BEING

A LITTLE PARABLE FOR MOTHERS

The young Mother set her foot on the path of life. "Is the way long?" she asked. And her Guide said, "Yes. And the way is hard. And you will be old before you reach the end of it. But the end will be better than the beginning."

But the young Mother was happy, and she would not believe that anything could be better than these years. So she played with her children, and gathered flowers for them along the way and bathed with them in the clear streams; and the sun shone on them, and life was good, and the young Mother cried, "Nothing will ever be lovelier than this."

Then came night, and storm, and the path was dark, and the children shook with fear and cold, and the Mother drew them close and covered them with her mantle, and the children said, "Oh, Mother, we are not afraid, for you are near, and no harm can come," and the Mother said, "This is better than the brightness of day, for I have taught my children courage."

And the next day came strange clouds which darkened the earth—clouds of war and hate and evil, and the children groped and stumbled, and the Mother said, "Look up. Lift your eyes to the Light." And the children looked and saw above the clouds an Everlasting Glory, and it guided them and brought them beyond the darkness. And that night, the Mother said, "This is the best day of all, for I have shown my children God."

And the days went on, and the weeks and months and the years, and the Mother grew old, and she was little and bent. But her children were tall and strong, and walked with courage. And when the way was hard, they helped their Mother; and when the way was rough, they lifted her, for she was as light as a feather; and at last they came to a hill, and beyond the hill they could see a shining road and golden gates flung wide.

And the Mother said, "I have reached the end of my journey. And now I know that the end is better than the beginning, for my children can walk alone, and their children after them."

And the children said, "You will always walk with us, Mother, even when you have gone through the gates."

And they stood and watched her as she went on alone, and the gates closed after her. And they said: "We cannot see her, but she is with us still. A Mother like ours is more than a memory. She is a Living Presence."

—Contributed by Temple Bailey[99]

LIVING FROM WITHIN

The story is told of a philosopher who stood at the gate of an ancient city greeting travelers who wished to enter. One of them questioned him:

"What kind of people live in your city?"

The philosopher met the question with a counter question: "What kind of people lived in the city from whence you came?"

"Oh, they were very bad people," answered the traveler, "cruel, deceitful, and devil-worshiping."

"That's the kind of people who live in this city," declared the philosopher. Then another traveler came by and asked the same question, to which the philosopher replied:

"What kind of people lived in the city from whence you came?"

"Oh, they were good people," answered the second traveler, "kind, truthful, and God-loving."

"That's the kind of people who live in this city," declared the philosopher.

—Contributed by Dr. David Goodman[100]

TO RUN AND NOT BE WEARY

When I was the president of the Cottonwood Stake, one of our stake patriarchs was Dr. Creed Haymond. He would occasionally bear strong testimony of the Word of Wisdom. As a young man he was the captain of the University of Pennsylvania track team. In 1919 Brother Haymond and his team were invited to participate in the annual Inter-Collegiate Association track meet. The night before the track meet, his coach, Lawson Robertson, who had coached several Olympic teams, instructed his team members to drink some sherry wine. In those days, coaches wrongly felt that wine was a tonic for muscles hardened through rigorous training. All the other team members took the sherry, but Brother Haymond refused because his parents had taught him the Word of Wisdom. Brother Haymond became very anxious because he did not like to be disobedient to his coach. He was to compete against the fastest men in the world. What if he made a poor showing the next day? How could he face his coach?

The next day at the track meet the rest of the team members were very ill and performed poorly or were even too sick to run. Brother Haymond, however, felt well and won the 100- and 220-yard dashes. His coach told him, "You just ran the two hundred and twenty yards in the fastest time it has ever been run by any human being." That night and for the rest of his life, Creed Haymond was grateful for his simple faith in keeping the Word of Wisdom.

—Contributed by James E. Faust[101]

YOUR MIND'S GARDEN

What seed have you sown in your garden of mind?
What thoughts have you sent into space?
Remember they yield you a harvest in kind
A life you henceforth must face.

For you are the sower, you choose your own seed
You fashion your future each day
Your garden is fertile, producing with speed
The fruit of each thought tucked away.

So if you wish happiness, health and peace
Then choose well each seed as you sow
Your future is shaped by the thoughts you release
Each hour, each day as you go.

—Elizabeth B. Waddel[102]

NINE REQUISITES
FOR CONTENTED LIVING

Health enough to make work a pleasure;
Wealth enough to support your needs;
Strength to battle with difficulties and overcome them;
Grace enough to confess your sins and forsake them;
Patience enough to toil until some good is accomplished;
Charity enough to see some good in your neighbor;
Love enough to move you to be useful and helpful to others;
Faith enough to make real the things of God;
Hope enough to remove all anxious fears concerning the future.

      —Johann Wolfgang von Goethe[103]

THE CHILDREN

When daily chores all are ended,
And playtime for the day is dismissed,
And the little ones gather around me
To say good-night prayers and be kissed,
Oh! the little white arms that encircle
My neck in a tender embrace!
Oh! the smiles that are haloes of Heaven
Shed sunshine of joy on my face!

When they're in their beds, I sit dreaming
Of my childhood, too lovely to last;
Of love that my heart well remembers
When it wakes to the pulse of the past
'Fore I noticed the mean things around me,
Unaware of sorrow and sin—
Then, the glory of God was about me,
And the glory of gladness within.

O! my heart goes back to my children
And my thoughts and feeling flow
As I think of the path, steep and stony,
Where the feet of my dear ones must go;
Of the mountains of sin hanging o'er them,
Of the tempest of fate flowing wild;
Oh! there's nothing on earth half so holy
As the innocent heart of a child.

They are idols of hearts and of household!
They are angels of God in disguise;
His sunlight still sleeps in their tresses,
His glory still gleams in their eyes;

These truants from home and from Heaven,
They have made me more gentle and mild;
And I know now how Jesus could liken
The kingdom of God to a child.

—Charles M. Dickinson[104]

No Man Is an Island

No man is an island;
No man stands alone.
Each man's joy is joy to me;
Each man's grief is my own.

We need one another,
So I will defend
Each man as my brother;
Each man as my friend.

I saw the people gather,
I heard the music start.
The song that they were singing
Is ringing in my heart.

No man is an island;
No man stands alone.
Each man's joy is joy to me;
Each man's grief my own.

We need one another,
So I will defend
Each man as my brother,
Each man as my friend.

—Adapted from sermon by John Donne[105]

Chapter Six
Spirituality Solution

To be spiritually-minded is life eternal.
—2 Nephi 9:39

Introduction for Parents

After much thought, I've decided that for this important section, I will share excerpts from a talk I presented in August 2002 for BYU Education Week in Provo, Utah. It was called "Teach children the Three R's: Respect, Responsibility, and Righteousness."

Do we teach the three R's of respect, responsibility, and righteousness as diligently as we teach reading, 'riting, and 'rithmetic? Think of Christ's original Twelve Apostles—unlearned by the standards of men but hand-picked by the Savior of the World for their goodness.

RESPECT

Respect means to esteem, treat with consideration, admire, and honor. The Lord thought this virtue was important enough to include in His Ten Commandments. "Honour thy father and thy mother: that thy days may be long upon the land" (Ex. 20:12).

I believe that the secret to having respectful children is to be the kind of fathers and mothers that children can respect. Now, it's true that whether a parent is worthy or not, there's a sense in which all children ought to honor their parents. But how much better it is when we live honorable lives before our children. Not perfect, but honorable lives.

I would like to suggest five ways we can be parents whom children honor and respect. We can love, lift, limit, lead, and laugh.

1. **Love**. The first way we can become parents worthy of being honored is by loving our children. One of the ways we can do that is by showing affection, even to our grown children. What did the father of the prodigal son do when his son came home after so much time away? He "fell on his neck, and kissed him" (Luke 15:20). This is a grown man with a grown son who had been living with the pigs! What a beautiful example of fatherly love! Jesus told that story with approval because that's the way a father is *supposed* to love.

We need to hug our kids often, supportively and tenderly. We should also hug them playfully, even when that teenage boy says, "Aw, Mom," and tries to pull away. Inside, he still wants you to hug him. Dads, you hug your boys too. It's healthy! Don't let the overly macho world of today tell you otherwise.

Our children long for our affection and appreciation. If we give it freely, they'll love our grandchildren better.

2. **Lift**. A second way to gain our children's respect is by lifting them up through encouragement. Colossians 3:21 of the holy Bible is a key verse here: "Fathers, provoke not your children to anger, lest they be discouraged."

I remember a time when we returned home from a trip and my formerly beautiful fern tree was just hanging over the edge of the pot, drooping and sad. Almost without hope for its recovery I gave it a big drink of water before going to bed that night. In the morning, I could hardly believe my eyes! My fern was upright and alive! Encouragement, given to children of any age, works the same way. Our children need lots of "lifts" in their lives to keep them emotionally healthy. Catch them doing things right and affirm the good things they do.

3.   **Limit.** In 1 Samuel 3:13, Heavenly Father said this about Eli: "I have told him that I will judge his house for ever for the iniquity which he knoweth; because his sons made themselves vile, and he restrained them not." Eli didn't set any limits for his boys, and it cost them all dearly.

When God put Adam and Eve in the garden, He gave them all they needed, but He also gave them limits. Our children *need* limits. Of course, they test those limits over and over. If we set reasonable limits, and if our children know we love them, they will feel secure when they push against the rules and those rules don't move.

Our society is being seduced away from the idea that life has limits or moral absolutes. Television sitcoms do this very well. They cause us to laugh at something, which means we don't take it seriously anymore. And if we can laugh at someone else's transgression, we won't take our own transgression seriously. So we have a generation that's laughing it's way down the wrong path.

We shouldn't be afraid to tell our children that particular movies, music, or television programs are absolutely unacceptable in our homes. They need to hear us set rules about immodest clothing, swearing, hitting, name-calling, etc. Then we need to teach them with consequences—kindly, firmly, and consistently.

4.   **Lead**. How can we be respected by our children? By *living* the principles we teach and expect them to live. It's called integrity—when our lives are in alignment with our values. What do we want our children to be? I don't mean their profession. I'm talking about their character. We must show them by our example what a man or woman of character looks like. Elder H. Burke Peterson said, "If our words are not consistent with our actions, they will never be heard" (*Ensign,* Nov. 1982, 43).

Adrian Rogers, the author of *Ten Secrets for a Successful Family,* told this story about a family friend who taught his son about respect:

> It seems that one of the boys lipped off to his mother one day. Now I don't know about your home, but in the Rogers' home showing disrespect to Mama was not tolerated. It wasn't tolerated in this home either, because the boy's father said to him, "Son, I want to tell you something. When you lipped off to your mother, you sinned against God. God says you are to honor her, and you're going to have to answer to Him for that.
>
> "Not only that, but you sinned against your mother. She went down into the valley of the shadow of death to bring you to life. How ungrateful you've been to speak to your mother that way, and you're going to have to answer to your mother for that."

And then this godly dad said, "I want to tell you something else. Not only is she your mother—she's my wife. And you're not going to talk that way to my wife. Now you not only have God and your mother to deal with, you've got me to deal with because you've shown disrespect to my wife."

Adrian Rogers finished, "I think that's one of the greatest training exercises I have ever heard in my life. . . . What a powerful impression a lesson like that would have on a young person.[106]

5. **Laugh.** Do we want to be honorable parents? We need to lighten up—learn how to laugh! Did you know that human beings are the only creatures of God who can laugh, weep, and blush? Our emotions are part of what it means to be made in God's image.

We should try to make our homes the happiest places on the block. Not long ago our son's friend joined our "movie night at the Fellingham house." After the movie my son David and our daughter Elise were quoting lines from movies they especially liked. We all laughed and laughed. When David came into the house after saying good-bye to his friend, he remarked, "She wants to know if she can come again to watch movies with us—and to laugh." If you don't have a sense of humor, how do you stay close to your teenagers?

Cartoonist Charles Schultz, the creator of Peanuts, said, "If I were given the opportunity to present a gift to the next generation, it would be the ability for each individual to learn to laugh at himself."[107]

Linda Ellerbee, of ABC News, said, "I have always felt that laughter in the face of reality is probably the finest sound there is and will last until the day when the game is called on account of darkness. In this world, a good time to laugh is any time you can."[108]

We just looked at things parents can do to be honored—respected—by their children. I'd like to quickly review several ways we can teach this virtue. I'm sure many of these things you do every day:

- Take care of your appearance. I think children (especially children over age eight) respect us more when we take care of ourselves physically. Sisters, even if we don't ever leave the house, each day we should be well groomed and look nice. It makes us feel better, too, doesn't it?
- Be cheerful and optimistic. Remember, it's a choice.
- Speak kindly. Use a gentle tone of voice.
- Eliminate sarcasm and criticism. It is so true that sarcastic humor damages relationships, and criticism kills them. We should try our best to eliminate both of them from our homes.
- Ask for your children's opinions. Show them their thoughts are valuable by encouraging them to participate in rule making and family decisions.
- Minimize the number of times you have to say no.
- Always be progressing mentally and spiritually.
- Set goals and work toward them.
- Treat your children's friends respectfully.
- Maintain high expectations of your children's behavior.

- Teach your children:
    - A. To respect their flag and their country
    - B. To respect their leaders (church, local, and national)
    - C. To respect their elders
    - D. To respect the rights of others
    - E. To respect all living things
    - F. To love their name, ancestors, and heritage
- Don't ever swear.
- Keep a (fairly) clean home.
- Be sincerely interested in what children enjoy ("know" their world).
- Support your children in their interests/hobbies.
- Communicate deeply with your children and listen to them. Having good communication skills is critical to successful parenting.
- Be there when your kids need you.
- Be flexible when necessary—adapt well to change.
- Be honest; never break children's trust.
- Have integrity. Let your life reflect your beliefs. When we compromise our standards and live contrary to what we preach, our children see us as hypocrites, and we lose a measure of their respect.

To close our discussion on respect, I'd like to share a story.

In 1994, workers doing some moving and remodeling at the Baseball Hall of Fame in Cooperstown, New York, discovered something rather unusual. As they were moving a display cabinet, they found an old photograph tucked behind the case. It was a photo of a stocky, friendly-looking man in a baseball uniform with the words "Sinclair Oil" on the shirt.

Stapled to the picture was a note in a man's scrawl that said, "You were never too tired to play ball. On your days off, you helped build the Little League field. You always came to watch me play. You were a Hall of Fame Dad. I wish I could share this moment with you."

No one knew how the picture got there or the identity of the man in the photo. A national sports magazine picked up the touching story, and a man came forward to say that he had tucked the picture and the note behind the display case during a visit to the Hall of Fame.

It seems the ballplayer in the photo was this man's late father. Just as the note said, this man was proud of his dad and believed he deserved to receive special recognition. So he decided to honor his father by holding his own little ceremony to induct him into the Hall of Fame.

—Contributed by Ben Fanton[109]

I want to be a Hall of Fame parent! Don't you? Let's be the kind of fathers and mothers who make it a joy and a delight for our children to obey God's command to "Honour thy father and thy mother."

RESPONSIBILITY

I'd like to talk about responsibility on two levels. The first has to do with taking responsibility for our thoughts, words, and actions. The second is about the importance of family work.

Years ago I had a life-changing experience. I imagine each one of you has had one of those—when something that someone said sunk deep in your heart, and because of it your perception or understanding changed forever.

I remember it so well. I was sitting on the front row of a lecture when the speaker quoted Eleanor Roosevelt: "No one can make you feel inferior without your consent."[106] The concept of taking responsibility for my own thoughts, words, and actions suddenly became crystal clear. Eleanor Roosevelt became one of my heroes that day as I internalized her message.

The concept is wonderful! We can *choose* what we think and how we act, no matter what is happening around us! When we're *responsible*, we no longer blame others or our circumstances for the way we act or the way we think. This is an incredibly important principle to teach our children. They *choose* their responses to life. The world might rain on them, but they can create a rainbow—and decide what color it's going to be!

The second level of responsibility has to do with work. A huge part of being an effective parent is teaching our children, from when they're very young, to be responsible. Young people who don't learn this principle go into the world handicapped. Give age-appropriate tasks and insist on a job well done. Whatever skills children learn (or don't learn) at home, they'll take those strengths (and weaknesses) with them when they leave us. Ask yourself this question: "What are my children's attitudes about work? How do *I* perceive it?"

When Adam and Eve left the garden, they exchanged an existence where life was sustained without effort for one dependent on hard work. Many have considered this need to labor as a curse, but a close reading of the Old Testament account suggests otherwise. God did not curse *Adam*. He cursed the *ground* to bring forth thorns and thistles, which in turn forced Adam to labor. Adam was told, "Cursed is the ground *for thy sake*" (Gen. 3:17, emphasis added). In other words, the hard work of eating one's bread "in the sweat of thy face" was meant to be a *blessing*.

How can work be a blessing? My good friend Dr. Kathleen Bahr addresses this question. In one of her insightful papers on family work she wrote,

> How does ordinary, family-centered work like feeding, clothing, and nurturing a family—work that often seems endless and mundane—actually bless our lives? Family work links people. On a daily basis, the tasks we do to stay alive provide us with endless opportunities to recognize and fill the needs of others. Family work is a call to enact love, and it is a call that is universal. Throughout history, in every culture, whether in poverty or prosperity, there has been the ever-present need to shelter, clothe, feed, and care for each other.
>
> Family work, by its very nature, can bind us to one another. Ironically, it is the very things commonly disliked about family work that offer the greatest possibilities for nurturing close relationships and forging family ties. Some people dislike family work because they say it is mindless. Yet, chores that can be done with a minimum of concentration leave our minds free to focus on one another as we work together. We can talk, sing, or tell stories as we work. Working side by side tends to dissolve feelings of

hierarchy, making it easier for children to discuss topics of concern with their parents. We also tend to think of household work as menial, and much of it is. Yet, because it's menial, even the smallest child can contribute.

Perhaps foremost, family work binds us together because it requires sacrifice. It demands that we put aside our own self-centered aims to see more clearly the needs of others.

Some people insist that family work is demeaning because it involves cleaning up after others in the most personal manner. Yet, in so doing, we observe their vulnerability and weaknesses, and we are reminded of our own dependence on others who have done, and will do, such work for us. We're reminded that when we are fed, we could be hungry; when we're clean, we could be dirty; and when we are healthy and strong, we could be feeble and dependent. Family work is thus humbling work . . . helping us acknowledge our interdependence, requiring us to sacrifice "self" for the good of the whole.

A frequent temptation in our busy lives today is to do work by ourselves. We've learned that it's usually more efficient to work alone. Also, we make our child responsible only for his own mess, to put away his own toys, to clean his own room, to do his own laundry, and then to consider this enough family work to require of a child. When we do this, we shortchange ourselves . . . we miss the growing together that comes from working together.

There was a study done with children from six cultures. African children showed the highest degree of helpfulness. They do family-care tasks like fetching wood or water, tending siblings, and running family errands. Children in the United States, whose primary task is to clean their own room, scored the lowest of the six cultures tested.

In America the activities of television, computer games, and recreation have made life so crowded that the virtues learned from family work are often neglected: service, sacrifice, love, respect, and mutual nurturing. I'll close this discussion on work with Wendell Berry's words: "In the face of prevailing fashion and opinion, my father showed remarkable insight and foresight. He insisted that I learn to do the hard labor that the land required, knowing—and saying again and again—that the ability to do such work is the source of a confidence and an independence of character that can come in no other way . . . not by money, not by education."[111]

RIGHTEOUSNESS

Elder Joseph B. Wirthlin defined righteousness well. He said, "Righteousness is living a life that is in harmony with the laws, principles, and ordinances of the gospel" (*Ensign,* May 1988, 81).

Elder Dean L. Larsen said, "The challenging conditions we find in the world today should be no surprise to us. As we approach the time of the Savior's return, wickedness will increase. There will be more temptations in our daily lives, and they will become more intense. It will become more acceptable in the world to break the laws of God or to disregard them altogether. The stigma attached to immoral, dishonest behavior will disappear" (*Ensign,* May 1983, 34).

Isn't that what's happening today? I mentioned the inclination of many to laugh at sin in sitcoms. How does the Lord teach? Line upon line, precept upon precept, here a little there a little. Don't we think Satan understands this? That's exactly how *he* teaches also. Little by little he leads people carefully down. He is patient, persistent, and subtle enough to do whatever is required to be occasionally, and then consistently, invited into our homes.

A wonderful representation of this concept was created by C. S. Lewis in an insightful fictional correspondence between an elderly devil, Screwtape, and his young nephew devil, Wormwood, who is just beginning his work of tempting mankind. Wormwood was complaining about his inability to tempt people into committing really big sins. He could only get them to commit "little" transgressions. His crafty and experienced Uncle Screwtape said,

> You will say that these are very small sins; and doubtless, like all young tempters, you are anxious to be able to report spectacular wickedness. But do remember, the only thing that matters is the extent to which you separate the man from the Enemy. It doesn't matter how small the sins are, provided that their cumulative effect is to edge the man away from the Light and out into the Nothing. Murder is no better than cards if cards can do the trick. Indeed, the safest road to Hell is the gradual one—the gentle slope, soft underfoot, without sudden turnings, without milestones, without signposts.[112]

How Satan would love to have our children turn from the Lord and follow him! He's working very hard now and succeeding with far too many of our young people. Our stewardship is to raise up a righteous generation unto the Lord. I believe that our challenge today of keeping our children *spiritually* alive is every bit as difficult as the challenge of the Saints of old as they worked to keep their children *physically* alive.

The following words should be taught to our youth over and over. They need to hear with clarity that evil and righteousness are black and white. President George Albert Smith said:

> There are two influences ever present in the world. One is constructive and elevating and comes from our Heavenly Father; the other is destructive and debasing and comes from Lucifer. We have our agency and make our own choice in life subject to these unseen powers. There is a division line well defined that separates the Lord's territory from Lucifer's. If we live on the Lord's side of the line Lucifer cannot come there to influence us, but if we cross the line into his territory, we are in his power. By keeping the commandments of the Lord we are safe on His side of the line, but if we disobey His teachings we voluntarily cross into the zone of temptation and invite the destruction that is ever present there. Knowing this, how anxious we should always be to live on the Lord's side of the line (*Improvement Era,* May 1935, 278).

And how can our children know what His side of the line is? How can they be sure they're always standing on the right side of the line? Moroni tells us:

> For behold, the Spirit of Christ is given to every man, that he may know good from evil; wherefore, I show unto you the way to judge; for every thing which inviteth to do good, and to persuade to believe in Christ, is sent forth by the power and gift of

Christ; wherefore ye may know with a perfect knowledge it is of God. But whatsoever thing persuadeth men to do evil, and believe not in Christ, and deny him, and serve not God, then ye may know with a perfect knowledge it is of the devil; for after this manner doth the devil work, for he persuadeth no man to do good, no, not one; neither do his angels; neither do they who subject themselves unto him (Moro. 7:16–17).

Speaking of the above scripture in Moroni, Elder Henry B. Eyring said,

I plead with you to take that [scripture] seriously. The world will become more wicked. You need the help of heaven to keep the commandments. You will need it more and more as the days go on. Satan will expand the space that is not safe. He will try every way he can to persuade you that there is no danger in trying to come as close as you can to that dividing line. At the same time, he is trying to persuade people that there really is no line at all. Because he knows that you know it is there, he will say to you, "Come closer to the line."

But you can bring the protective powers of heaven down on you simply by deciding to go toward the Savior . . . Satan will tell you, as he has done regularly for ages, that you will not be happy in safety, that you must come near his ground to live the happy life. Well, that is a clear choice, too.[113]

Following are twelve ways we can teach our children to be righteous:

1. *Set a good example.* Model Christ's attributes. Let's take just one—compassion. We *want* our children to be the ones to rush to the side of a hurt friend, to be the children who notice and help less-fortunate classmates. If they watch us show little acts of kindness and compassion, they'll follow our example. This is true for every virtue.

2. *Create a home atmosphere that invites the Spirit of the Lord.* What do your children see in your home? Do you have pictures of the temple and the Savior in your home? Are the Ten Commandments or the thirteen Articles of Faith hanging on your walls? What else do your children see? Let's talk about the effects that the media in our house have on our children. Movies, television, video games, the Internet—these things are like double-edged swords. For example, there are marvelous and wonderful things to learn on the Internet, but parts of cyberspace are the devil's playground.

It is our stewardship as parents to teach our children how to use media as tools for righteousness and avoid the pitfalls they provide. Elder M. Russell Ballard said,

Remember, there is no such thing as unlawful censorship in the home. Movies, magazines, television, videos, the Internet, and other media are there as guests and should only be welcomed when they are appropriate for family enjoyment. Make your home a haven of peace and righteousness. Don't allow evil influences to contaminate your own special spiritual environment (*Ensign*, May 1999, 87).

President Gordon B. Hinckley remarked,

> We live in an age of compromise and acquiescence. In situations with which we are daily confronted, we know what is right, but under pressure from our peers and the beguiling voices of those who would persuade us, we capitu late. We compromise. We acquiesce. We give in, and we are ashamed of ouselves. . . . we must cultivate the strength to follow our convictions!" (*Ensign*, Nov. 1992, 52).

President Hinckley also said,

> The time has come for us to stand a little taller, to lift our eyes and stretch our minds to a greater comprehension and understanding of the grand millennial mission of this The Church of Jesus Christ of Latter-day Saints. This is a season to be strong. It is a time to move forward without hesitation, knowing well the meaning, the breadth, and the importance of our mission. It is a time to do what is right regardless of the consequences that might follow. It is a time to be found keeping the commandments. It is a time . . . to become more Christlike" (*Ensign*, May 1995, 71).

3. *Choose your friends and neighborhood carefully.* Friends are powerful influences for both good and evil. Choose your neighborhood carefully. Victor B. Cline in his book *Make Your Child A Winner* writes,

> Whether you like it or not, the children our youngsters choose as their friends will have an increasingly significant impact upon their lives, values and behavior—especially as they get older and move into their adolescent years. . . . This means you should choose the neighborhood you live in at least as carefully as you choose your particular house; the neighborhood will provide the peer culture for your children as they grow up and that might make a critically important difference in their lives.[114]

4. *Read the scriptures.* President Marion G. Romney testified of the blessings that will come to those who study the scriptures, especially the Book of Mormon:

> I feel certain that if, in our homes, parents will read from the Book of Mormon prayerfully and regularly, both by themselves and with their children, the spirit of that great book will come to permeate our homes and all who dwell therein. The spir it of reverence will increase; mutual respect and consideration for each other will grow. The spirit of contention will depart. Parents will counsel their children in greater love and wisdom. Children will be more responsive and submissive to the counsel of their parents. Righteousness will increase. Faith, hope and charity—the pure love of Christ—will abound in our homes and lives, bringing in their wake peace, joy, and happiness" (*Ensign*, May 1980, 67).

5. *Hold family home evening.* In 1915 the Prophet Joseph F. Smith and his coun-

selors in the First Presidency made this promise to families who hold regular family home evenings: "If the Saints obey this counsel, we promise that great blessings will result. Love at home and obedience to parents will increase. Faith will be developed in the hearts of the youth of Israel, and they will gain power to combat the evil influence and temptations which beset them."[115]

6. *Pray individually and with the family.* President Gordon B. Hinckley said,

> Let every family in this Church have prayer together. Now, it is important to have individual prayer, but it is a wonderful thing to have family prayer. Pray to your Father in Heaven in faith. Pray in the name of the Lord Jesus Christ. You can do nothing better for your children than to have them taking their turn in the family prayer, expressing gratitude for their blessings. If they do that while they are young, they will grow with a spirit of thanksgiving in their hearts (*Ensign*, Aug. 1997, 5).

7. *Attend Church services and Church activities.* Attending church together, as a family, is an issue of obedience. In my mind, it is never an option for children. We obey.

8. *Keep the Sabbath holy.*

9. *Set the rules **with** your children.* Then discuss consequences for obedience and disobedience to the rules.

10. *Discipline with love.* The three keys to effective discipline are kindness, firmness, and consistency.

11. *Work together.*

12. *Play together.*

We go to college to become a lawyer, educator, nurse, etc. We come to this earth-school to become like Christ. The Savior asked, "Therefore, what manner of men ought ye to be? Verily I say unto you, even as I am" (3 Ne. 27:27).

Knowing, as we do, that example is the best way to teach children, it behooves us to be what we want them to become. What we and our children need is a spiritual change of heart, which we can enjoy right now, in this life. Former BYU President Merrill Bateman said, "The greatest miracle of the Atonement is the power Jesus Christ has to change our character if we come to Him with a broken heart and a contrite spirit" (*Ensign*, Jan. 1999, 12–13).

We want our children's hearts to be soft. What are some of the things we can do to help keep our children loving and teachable, the way they came to us?

- Hold them close when they're tiny. Be there when they need you—be patient.
- Hold them close when they're young. Teach them what God has commanded us to teach them: to love and serve one another.

- Hold them close when they're older. Prepare them well for life, for going to the temple, for eternal marriage.
- Yes, and when they're older, just like when they were young, be there when they need you—and be patient.

What about parenting hard-hearted children? In spite of, and after, parents' best efforts, some children make decisions that cause great sorrow for themselves and others. Parents must never cease to love children who go astray. Elder Richard G. Scott said, "Some of you have children that do not respond to you, choosing entirely different paths. Father in Heaven has repeatedly had that same experience. While some of His children have used His gift of agency to make choices against His counsel, He continues to love them. Yet, I am sure, He has never blamed Himself for their unwise choices" (*Ensign,* May 1993, 34).

While serving in the Quorum of the Twelve Apostles, Elder Howard W. Hunter gave the following counsel to parents who have done their best but grieve because of the mistakes of a child:

> A successful parent is one who has loved, one who has sacrificed, and one who has cared for, taught, and ministered to the needs of a child. If you have done all of these and your child is still wayward or troublesome or worldly, it could well be that you are, nevertheless, a successful parent. Perhaps there are children who have come into the world that would challenge any set of parents under any set of circumstances. Likewise, perhaps there are others who would bless the lives of, and be a joy to, almost any father or mother (*Ensign,* Nov. 1983, 65).

Elder Richard G. Scott said,

> When I take a small pebble and place it directly in front of my eye, it takes on the appearance of a mighty boulder. It is all I can see. It becomes all-consuming—like the problems of a loved one that affect our lives every waking moment. When the things you realistically can do to help are done, leave the matter in the hands of the Lord and worry no more. Do not feel guilty because you cannot do more. Do not waste your energy on useless worry. The Lord will take the pebble that fills your vision and cast it down among the challenges you will face in your eternal progress. It will then be seen in perspective. In time, you will feel impressions and know how to get further help. You will find more peace and happiness, will not neglect others that need you, and will be able to give greater help because of that eternal perspective (*Ensign,* May 1988, 60).

I'll close with a poem read by President Thomas S. Monson in the general conference of October 1993:

> He stood at the crossroads all alone,
> The sunlight in his face.
> He had no thought for the world unknown—
> He was set for a manly race.
> But the roads stretched east, and the roads stretched west,
> And the lad knew not which road was best;
> So he chose the road that led him down,

And he lost the race and victor's crown.
He was caught at last in an angry snare
Because no one stood at the crossroads there
To show him the better road.

Another day, at the self-same place,
A boy with high hopes stood.
He, too, was set for a manly race;
He, too, was seeking the things that were good;
But one was there who the roads did know,
And that one showed him which way to go.
So he turned from the road that would lead him down,
And he won the race and the victor's crown.
He walks today the highway fair
Because one stood at the crossroads there
To show him the better way.

—Author Unknown (*Ensign*, Nov. 1993, 48).

May we be there for our children to teach them respect, responsibility, and righteousness. May we "walk the highway fair" because One has stood—for ages—at the crossroads there, showing us the better way. Let it be our joy to seek to emulate Him each day of our lives.

Lesson Twenty-One
Believe

It is in the home that we form our attitudes, our deeply held beliefs.

—President Thomas S. Monson (*Ensign*, Nov. 1999, 19)

FOLLOW-UP

(As a family, discuss the assignment for the lesson "Financial Well-Being.")

1. What are some of the things we're doing to live within our budget?
2. What steps are we taking to save some of our money?

CONCEPT

Believing in God means that we believe there is a Father in Heaven who loves us. We believe that Heavenly Father exists, even though we haven't seen Him. We believe there is a wonderful "master plan" for this world and its people.

Heavenly Father loves us and He wants us to be happy. Believing this gives us faith that God cares about us individually and as a family. We trust that Heavenly Father and Jesus Christ will help us when we turn to Them in prayer.

Elder Bruce R. McConkie said, "Belief, humble belief, is the foundation of all righteousness and the beginning of spiritual progression."[116] Families can enjoy eternal peace and happiness when they act on their beliefs by keeping Heavenly Father's commandments and living the principles of the gospel.

When the Prophet Joseph Smith was asked what members of The Church of Jesus Christ of Latter-day Saints believe, he answered by writing the Articles of Faith. Let's read these beliefs:

The Articles of Faith

1. We believe in God, the Eternal Father, and in His Son, Jesus Christ, and in the Holy Ghost.
2. We believe that men will be punished for their own sins, and not for Adam's transgression.

3. We believe that through the Atonement of Christ, all mankind may be saved, by obedience to the laws and ordinances of the Gospel.

4. We believe that the first principles and ordinances of the Gospel are: first, Faith in the Lord Jesus Christ; second, Repentance; third, Baptism by immersion for the remission of sins; fourth, Laying on of hands for the gift of the Holy Ghost.

5. We believe that a man must be called of God, by prophecy, and by the laying on of hands by those who are in authority, to preach the Gospel and administer in the ordinances thereof.

6. We believe in the same organization that existed in the Primitive Church, namely, apostles, prophets, pastors, teachers, evangelists, and so forth.

7. We believe in the gift of tongues, prophecy, revelation, visions, healing, interpretation of tongues, and so forth.

8. We believe the Bible to be the word of God as far as it is translated correctly; we also believe the Book of Mormon to be the word of God.

9. We believe all that God has revealed, all that He does now reveal, and we believe that He will yet reveal many great and important things pertaining to the Kingdom of God.

10. We believe in the literal gathering of Israel and in the restoration of the Ten Tribes; that Zion (the New Jerusalem) will be built upon the American continent; that Christ will reign personally upon the earth; and, that the earth will be renewed and receive its paradisiacal glory.

11. We claim the privilege of worshiping Almighty God according to the dictates of our own conscience, and allow all men the same privilege, let them worship how, where, or what they may.

12. We believe in being subject to kings, presidents, rulers, and magistrates, in obeying, honoring, and sustaining the law.

13. We believe in being honest, true, chaste, benevolent, virtuous, and in doing good to all men; indeed, we may say that we follow the admonition of Paul—We believe all things, we hope all things, we have endured many things, and hope to be able to endure all things. If there is anything virtuous, lovely, or of good report or praiseworthy, we seek after these things.

FAMILY SURVEY REVIEW
Statement 21: We believe and live the principles of the gospel.

- Is it harder to live the gospel than to believe it is true?
- Name one commandment that our family always obeys.

STORY

President Thomas S. Monson told this story:

On my first visit to the fabled village of Sauniatu in Samoa, so loved by President McKay, my wife and I met with a large gathering of small children. At the end of our messages to these shy, beautiful youngsters, I suggested to the native Samoan teacher that we go ahead with the closing exercises. As he announced the closing hymn, I suddenly felt compelled to greet personally each of the 247 children. But the time was too short for such a privilege, so I ignored the impression. Before the benediction, however, I again felt this strong impression to shake the hand of each child. I told the teacher that I wanted to shake the hand of each child. He displayed a broad Samoan smile before relaying my intentions in Samoan to the children. They all beamed when they heard his translation.

The teacher then told me the special reason for their joy. He said, "When we learned that President McKay had assigned a member of the Quorum of the Twelve to visit us in faraway Samoa, I told the children that if each one would earnestly and sincerely pray and exert faith like in the Bible accounts of old, the Apostle would visit our tiny village at Sauniatu, and through their faith, he would be impressed to greet each child with a personal handclasp." Tears flowed as each of those precious boys and girls walked by and whispered softly to us a sweet *talofa lava* (hello). The gift of faith had been evidenced (*Friend*, Nov. 1987, inside front cover).

DISCUSSION

1. Why did President Monson feel inspired to shake each individual child's hand?
2. What are some ways that you show belief in Heavenly Father?

ACTIVITY

As individuals and as a family, we should try to live the higher law and show love to all of our fellowmen. If we do this, one of the blessings that will follow is a greater desire to serve others. We are God's hands on earth.

The activity for this lesson is to choose a person or a family we can serve and to do an act of kindness for them. Let's decide what to do, then plan the activity. If we can serve others without them knowing it, all the better!

ASSIGNMENT

Read the story below, called "Belief," and do one or more of the suggestions listed in Additional Solution for Success that follows this lesson.

Sir Isaac Newton, the British scientist, once had a skillful mechanic make him a miniature replica of our solar system with balls representing the planets. [It was] geared together by cogs and belts so as to move in harmony when cranked. Later, Newton was visited by a scientist friend who did not believe in God.

As Newton sat reading in his study with his mechanism on a large table near him, his friend stepped in. Scientist that he was, he recognized at a glance what was before him. Stepping up to it he slowly turned the crank, and with undisguised admiration watched the heavenly bodies all move in their relative speed in their orbits. Standing off a few feet he exclaimed, "My! What an exquisite thing this is! Who made it?" Without looking up from his book, Newton answered, "Nobody."

Quickly turning to Newton, the man said, "Evidently you did not understand the question. I asked who made this?" Looking up now, Newton solemnly assured him that nobody made it, but that the aggregation of matter so much admired had just happened to assume the form it was in. But the astonished scientist replied with some heat, "You must think I am a fool! Of course somebody made it, and he is a genius, and I'd like to know who he is."

Laying aside his book, Newton arose and laid a hand on his friend's shoulder. "This thing is but a puny imitation of a much grander system whose laws you know, and I am not able to convince you that this mere toy is without a designer and maker; yet you profess to believe that the great original from which the design is taken has come into being without either designer or maker! Now tell me by what sort of reasoning do you reach such an incongruous conclusion?"[117]

ADDITIONAL SOLUTION FOR SUCCESS
SPIRITUALITY

1. Pray together as a family each night and morning.

2. Read scriptures regularly as a family.

3. Hold family home evening every week.

4. Spend some time alone in nature thinking about Heavenly Father and your mission on earth.

5. Sing or listen to beautiful songs that tell of God and His goodness.

6. Learn more about a specific gospel topic.

7. Attend Church meetings as a family.

8. Do an anonymous act of kindness for another family.

9. Share the gospel with friends.

10. Make a long list of your blessings. Talk about how much your family has to be grateful for.

Lesson Twenty-Two
Pray

Prayer is the key which unlocks the door and lets Christ into our lives.

—Elder Marion G. Romney (*Ensign*, May 1978, 50)

FOLLOW-UP

(As a family, discuss the assignment for the lesson "Believe.")

1. What was the activity we did from the Additional Solution for Success list from the last lesson?
2. What did we learn from this activity?

CONCEPT

Prayer is communicating with Heavenly Father. It is an act of worship that should include both talking and listening. The unspoken yearnings of our hearts that go up in supplication to God are also prayers. The formalities of *what* we say and *how* we say it are not as important as the act of reaching out to Heavenly Father in faith that He will hear us.

President Gordon B. Hinckley encouraged us to "Believe in the power of prayer. Believe in getting on your knees every morning and every night and talking with your Father in Heaven concerning the feelings of your hearts and the desires of your minds in righteousness. There is no power upon the earth like the power of prayer."[118]

Our Father in Heaven wants to help us, and He will help us in accordance with His great wisdom and love, His knowledge of our true needs, and our desire for His help.

Jesus Christ taught us how to pray. During His earthly ministry, Jesus' disciples were often with Him when He prayed. They wanted to know how to pray, so they asked, "Lord, teach us to pray" (Luke 11:1). Jesus kindly responded to their request and taught them:

Our Father which art in heaven, Hallowed be thy name. Thy kingdom come. Thy will be done in earth as it is in heaven. Give us this day our daily bread. And forgive us our debts, as we forgive our debtors. And lead us not into temptation, but deliver us from evil: For thine is the kingdom, and the power, and the glory for ever. Amen (Matt. 6:9–13).

In the Doctrine and Covenants the Lord says, "Pray always, and I will pour out my Spirit upon you, and great shall be your blessing" (D&C 19:38).

Four steps of prayer are suggested:

1. *Prepare.* As we prepare to speak to Heavenly Father, we should try to rid our mind of worldly thoughts and focus on Him. For a moment we should contemplate His greatness and goodness and think about what we'll say in our prayer.

2. *Express gratitude.* The second part of a prayer is to praise Heavenly Father and thank Him for His blessings to us and to our family. We should thank God for specific things, expressing gratitude with all of our hearts.

3. *Ask for help.* We should pray for specific ways Heavenly Father can help us, and seek forgiveness for our wrongdoings.

4. *Listen.* Part of prayer is seeking to know God's will for us. How can we learn His will if we don't listen? We should keep our minds open and believing. During and after our prayers we should pause and listen, trying sincerely to receive insights that may help us. Divine impressions will come more readily when we're quietly listening.

FAMILY SURVEY REVIEW
Statement 22: Our family prays together.

- Do you think Heavenly Father hears and answers prayers?
- When should we pray?

STORY

Once there was an injured little orphan boy who was hurried to the hospital where it was determined that he needed an immediate operation. When he was wheeled into the operating room, he heard the doctors and nurses discussing his problem. He knew that it was very serious. The young boy spoke to a doctor as they were preparing to give him the anesthetic. "Doctor, before you begin to operate, will you please pray for me?"

The doctor, with seeming embarrassment, said, "I can't pray for you." The boy asked the other doctor, with the same result. Then the little boy said, "If you can't pray for me, will you please wait while I pray for myself?"

They removed the sheet, and he knelt on the operating table. He bowed his head and said, "Heavenly Father, I am just an orphan boy, and I'm awful sick. Won't you please make me well? Bless these men who are going to operate that they'll do it right. If you will make me well, I'll try to grow up and be a good man. Thank you. In the name of Jesus Christ, Amen."

When the little boy was finished, he lay down. The doctors' and nurses' eyes were filled with tears. The child said, "I'm ready now."

The operation was performed. The boy was taken back to his room, and before long he was well on his way to recovery.

Sometime afterward the experienced surgeon remarked, "I have operated on hundreds of people, men and women who thought they had faith to be healed. But never until I stood over that little boy have I felt the Spirit of God as I felt it then. That boy opened the windows of heaven and talked to his God as one would have talked to his friend, face-to-face. I want to say to you that I am a better man for having heard a little boy pray."[119]

DISCUSSION

1. Why did the little boy want to pray?
2. How did the surgeon feel about the boy's prayer?
3. Do you believe Heavenly Father hears your prayers?

ACTIVITY

The activity for this lesson is to gather together and say a prayer as a family.

ASSIGNMENT

The assignment is to lift your thoughts to Heavenly Father and Jesus Christ often and include Them in your lives through prayer.

Also, read the Additional Solution for Success: The Healing Power of Prayer.

ADDITIONAL SOLUTION FOR SUCCESS
THE HEALING POWER OF PRAYER

This interesting discovery concerning prayer was reported by Dr. Larry Dossey in *Reader's Digest* in March 1996:

It was during residency training at Parkland Memorial Hospital in Dallas, Texas, when I had my first patient with terminal cancer in both lungs. I advised him on what therapy was available and what little I thought it would do. Rightly enough, he opted for no treatment.

Yet whenever I stopped by his hospital bedside, he was surrounded by visitors from his church, singing and praying. *Good thing,* I thought, *because soon they'll be singing and praying at his funeral.*

A year later, when I was working elsewhere, a colleague at Parkland called to ask if I wanted to see my old patient. *See him?* I couldn't believe he was still alive. I studied his chest X rays and was stunned. The man's lungs were completely clear—there was no sign of cancer.

"His therapy has been remarkable," the radiologist said, looking over my shoulder.

Therapy? I thought. *There wasn't any—unless you consider prayer. . . .*

I had long ago given up the faith of my childhood. Now I believed in the power of modern medicine. Prayer seemed an arbitrary frill, so I put the incident out of my mind.

The years passed, and I became chief of staff at a large urban hospital. I was aware that many of my patients used prayer, but I put little trust in it. Then, in the late '80s I began to come across studies—many conducted under stringent laboratory conditions—which showed that prayer had brought about significant changes in a variety of physical conditions.

Perhaps the most convincing study, published in 1988, was by cardiologist Dr. Randolph Byrd. A computer assigned 393 patients, at the coronary-care unit of San Francisco General Hospital, either to a group that was prayed for by prayer groups or to a group that was not remembered in prayer. No one knew which group the patients were in. The prayer groups were simply given the patients' first names, along with brief descriptions of their medical problems. They were asked to pray each day until the patient was discharged from the hospital—but were given no instructions on how to do it or what to say.

When the study was completed ten months later, the prayed-for patients benefited in several significant areas:

- They were five times less likely than the unremembered group to require antibiotics.
- They were two times less likely to suffer congestive heart failure.
- They were less likely to suffer cardiac arrest.

If the medical technique being studied had been a new drug or surgical procedure instead of prayer, it would probably have been heralded as a breakthrough. Even hard-boiled skeptics like Dr. William Nolen, who had written a book questioning the validity of faith healing, acknowledged, "If this is a valid study, we doctors ought to be writing on our order sheets, 'Pray three times a day.' If it works, it works."

I have since given up practicing medicine to devote myself to researching and writing about prayer and how it affects our health. There are studies which suggest that prayer can have a beneficial effect on high blood pressure, wounds, headaches, and anxiety. Here are some of the things I've found:

- **Prayer Can Take Many Forms.** In the studies I've seen, results occurred not only when people prayed for explicit outcomes but also when they prayed for nothing specific. Some studies, in fact, showed that a simple "Thy will be done" was quantitatively more powerful than specific results held in the mind. In many experiments a simple attitude of prayerfulness—an all-pervading sense of holiness and a feeling of empathy, caring and compassion—seemed to set the stage for healing.

- **Love Increases the Power of Prayer.** The power of love is legendary. It's built into folklore, common sense, and everyday experience. . . . Throughout history, tender, loving care has uniformly been recognized as a valuable element in healing. In fact, a survey of 10,000 men with heart disease, published in *The American Journal of Medicine*, found close to a fifty percent reduction in frequency of angina in those who perceived their wives as supportive and loving. . . .

- **Prayer Can Be Open-Ended.** Most people who pray are convinced that it can be used in a purposeful, goal-specific manner. But research shows that open-ended entreaties seem to work too. Invocations such as "Thy will be done," "Let it be" or "May the best thing happen" do not involve "using" prayer for specific outcomes, nor do they involve sending complicated messages.

  Perhaps this is what some people mean when they advocate, "Let go and let God." Many recognize in their own prayers a spontaneous, uncontrollable quality that brings results.

- **Prayer Means You Are Not Alone.** A patient of mine was dying. The day before his death, I sat at his bedside with his wife and children. He knew he had little time left, and he chose his words carefully, speaking in a hoarse whisper. Although he was not a religious person, he revealed to us that recently he had begun to pray. "What do you pray *for*?" I asked him.

  "It isn't 'for' anything," he said thoughtfully. "It simply reminds me that I am not alone."[120]

Lesson Tewnty-Three
Worship

There is something essential about joining together with other believers to worship, to sing, to pray, to learn of God's will for us, and to acknowledge his goodness to us. He has commanded that this should be so.

—Elder Dean L. Larsen (*Ensign*, Nov. 1989, 63)

FOLLOW-UP

(As a family, discuss the assignment for the lesson "Pray.")

1. Have we been praying both night and morning?
2. While we're praying, and after praying, how do we feel?

CONCEPT

Worship is the act or feeling of adoration and devotion, the paying of religious reverence as in prayer, praise, etc. Jesus Christ said, "Thou shalt worship the Lord thy God, and him only shalt thou serve" (Luke 4:8).

And Nephi counseled us, "Ye must bow down before [Christ], and worship him with all your might, mind, and strength, and your whole soul" (2 Ne. 25:29). What do you think Nephi meant when he wrote that?

Here are some ways we can worship our Heavenly Father and Jesus Christ:

- *Prayer:* Communicating with Heavenly Father in Christ's name.

- *Meditation:* Thinking deeply about spiritual things.

- *Church Attendance:* Renewing covenants and learning gospel principles.

- *Music:* Listening to and creating uplifting music, bringing thoughts of divinity, gratitude, and love.

- *Scripture Reading:* Feasting on the words of the Lord.

- *Temple Attendance:* Participating as often as possible in temple ordinances.

President Hinckley promised, "Every time you come to the temple, you will be a better man or woman when you leave than you were when you came. I believe that with all my heart. Redouble your efforts and your faithfulness in going to the temple . . . and the Lord will bless you, and you will be happier" (*Ensign,* Mar. 2001, 65).

Think about the definition of worship as feelings of adoration and devotion. Does that describe how we feel about some of our possessions or activities in life? There are people who care so much about the accumulation of wealth or power that they neglect family relationships. Some people adore money, a large house, or an expensive car. Is that what they worship? We may want to reflect on what it is that we worship. Spending time learning about Heavenly Father and the gospel of Jesus Christ, and nurturing a loving, righteous family is far more important than spending time accumulating more money than is necessary.

One final thought about worship comes from Elder Bruce R. McConkie. During an address to the students at Brigham Young University, he explained: "The Lord is saying to us, 'Here is how you worship. You worship by emulation. You worship by imitation. You worship by patterning your life after mine. You worship by magnifying me and my course, by doing what I have done.'"[121]

FAMILY SURVEY REVIEW
Statement 23: We worship Heavenly Father as a family.

- How do we worship Heavenly Father and Jesus Christ in our family?
- How can we worship with more dedication?

STORY

Once upon a time there were three men who were told they would have an interview in which they'd be asked to tell what they knew about God.

The first man entered the room and described to the interviewer in great detail all he had learned about God. He told about God's great wisdom and His omnipotent power. The man then described God's love and compassion. The interviewer listened with intense interest while the first man spoke. When the man was finished, the interviewer thanked him sincerely and excused him.

The second man entered the room. This gentleman was well learned and regarded as an expert in religion. He began by explaining several different theories about God. This second man was well prepared for the interview and presented a lengthy discourse on the Almighty. The interviewer listened attentively, then thanked the man for his time. The knowledgeable gentleman left the room.

The third man entered. As he looked into the face of the interviewer, he immediately fell to his knees and exclaimed, "My Lord, my God!"

The first two men knew many things about God. The third man knew God.[122]

DISCUSSION

1. When people worship, they can either give "lip service" (say the words without really meaning it), or they can worship Heavenly Father and Jesus Christ with their whole hearts and show by their actions what they believe. Do we give "lip service" or do we worship with our whole heart?
2. What can we do to improve in this area of spirituality?

ACTIVITY

Our activity for this lesson is to attend our Church meetings as a family and then talk about what each family member learned.

ASSIGNMENT

Read the Additional Solution for Success: Worship Through Music.

ADDITIONAL SOLUTION FOR SUCCESS
WORSHIP THROUGH MUSIC

Well-known composer Igor Stravinsky (1882–1971) proclaimed, "Music praises God. Music is as well or better able to praise Him than the building of the church and all its decorations; it is the church's greatest ornament."[123] Indeed, music can be a powerful form of worship. It has been called the universal language, the language of God.

Many believe that God has inspired composers through the ages as they've created beautiful music. Stravinsky asserted, "Only God can create. I make music from music."[124] He stated also, "I regard my talents as God-given, and I have always prayed to Him for strength to use them."[125]

Composer Ludwig van Beethoven (1770–1827) believed in God and His power to help him compose. He recorded his thoughts: "It was not a fortuitous meeting of chordal atoms that made the world; if order and beauty are reflected in the constitution of the universe, then there is a God. . . . Therefore, calmly will I submit myself to all inconsistency and will place all my confidence in your eternal goodness, O God!"[126]

Haydn also acknowledged God's hand in his work:

> On March 27, 1808, Franz Joseph Haydn attended his last musical performance. The program featured his oratorio *The Creation*. He'd finished the massive work at age sixty-six, saying it had been composed to inspire "the adoration and worship of the Creator" and to put the listener "in a frame of mind where he is most susceptible to the kindness and omnipotence of the Creator." Haydn recalled, "Never was I so devout as when I composed *The Creation*. I knelt down each day to pray to God to give me strength for my work." He told a friend, "When I was working on *The Creation*, I felt so impregnated with the Divine certainty that, before sitting down to the piano, I would quietly and confidently pray to God to grant me the talent that was needed to praise Him worthily." At this March 1808 performance of his triumphant oratorio, the composer was determined that God would get all the glory for his work. As the music faded and the audience applauded enthusiastically, Haydn lifted his hands and said, "Not from me—from there, above, comes everything."[127]

Another great composer, Wolfgang Amadeus Mozart (1756–1791), also professed his belief in, and reliance upon, God. Mozart once wrote, "Let us put our trust in God and console ourselves with the thought that all is well, if it is in accordance with the will of the Almighty, as He knows best what is profitable and beneficial to our temporal happiness and our eternal salvation."[128]

Johann Sebastian Bach (1685–1750) also believed God and good music to be inseparable. Bach was a career church musician in Germany. He proclaimed, "Music's only purpose should be for the glory of God and the recreation of the human spirit."[129]

George Frederick Handel (1685–1759), a contemporary of Bach, believed fervently that God intervened and assisted in the creation of music:

> In 1741, Handel was genuinely discouraged. His health was failing, audiences had deserted him, and he was deeply in debt. Seeing no hope for the future, his music, or his life, he was ready to retire in disgrace. It seems that God had other plans for

Handel. Two challenges almost simultaneously set before him changed his life and the map of the musical world. From a Dublin charity, he received a commission to compose a piece of music for a benefit concert. From Charles Jennings, a wealthy friend, he received a libretto based exclusively on Bible texts.

With that libretto in hand, Handel went into a feverish work mode. For three weeks, beginning on August 22, he confined himself to his small house on Brook Street in London. From early morning into the night, he rarely left his music paper, ink, and pens. A friend who visited at that time reported having seen Handel weeping with intense emotion. Later, as Handel related the compositional experience, he quoted St. Paul's words: "Whether I was in the body or out of my body when I wrote it, I know not."

At one point a servant came into Handel's room to deliver a tray of food. He reported having seen a wild expression in his employer's eyes; a weeping Handel refused the food and exclaimed, "I did think I did see all Heaven before me, and the great God Himself." He had just completed what has become the most-performed choral movement in history, the "Hallelujah Chorus."

After six days of this incredibly concentrated work, Handel had completed Part 1. Part 2 took him nine days, and Part 3 took another six. In two more days—to complete the orchestration—the masterpiece called the *Messiah* was finished. In the unbelievably brief span of twenty-four days, Handel had filled two hundred sixty pages of manuscript. . . . Musicologist Robert Myers has stated that the music and its powerful message "has probably done more to convince thousands of mankind that there is a God about us than all the theological works ever written."[130]

Yes, music is a powerful form of worship. Bach wrote in the margin of a biblical commentary, "Where there is devotional music, God is always at hand with his gracious presence."[131]

Additionally, we learn from the Apostle Mark that, in the upper room, as Jesus was preparing to sacrifice His life, He and His disciples prepared for the ordeal by singing a hymn. "And when they had sung an hymn, they went out into the mount of Olives" (Mark 14:26). In Doctrine and Covenants 25:12, we learn how Christ enjoys music: "For my soul delighteth in the song of the heart; yea, the song of the righteous is a prayer unto me, and it shall be answered with a blessing upon their heads."

Lesson Twenty-Four
Share

Our Heavenly Father gave His Son. The Son of God gave His life. We are asked by Them to give our lives . . . in Their divine service. Will you? Will I? Will we? There are lessons to be taught, there are kind deeds to be done, there are souls to be saved.
—President Thomas S. Monson (*Ensign*, Nov. 1999, 20)

FOLLOW-UP

(As a family, discuss the assignment for the lesson "Worship.")

1. Did we discuss what we learned at church last week? If not, what did we learn?
2. What did the last lesson teach us about ways to worship Heavenly Father and Jesus Christ?

CONCEPT

Share is an action word that means to give a portion of what we have, or who we are, to others. For example, when someone has a problem, we can give of ourselves by listening to them, and discussing possible solutions. If someone needs knowledge, a helping hand, or an understanding heart, we can share ours.

We can share our positive attitude by smiling and being friendly. We can look for opportunities to share our time and energy. We can forgive. We can love all people. There are countless ways to share.

There is a saying, "Giving is its own reward—all that we send into the lives of others comes back into our own." It is a true principle that when we give, we also receive. Just as a successful farmer harvests after planting, we also reap rewards of joy when we unselfishly share our possessions, time, talents, and strengths with others.

Just as a person in darkness appreciates another's light, so we can help others by sharing our spiritual light. How can we do this? To share a light, we must first have one. Believing, praying, learning, and worshiping are ways to increase our understanding of God and to create that "light." Additionally, when we obey God's laws, show love to everyone, and tirelessly serve others, we will earn a light to share. At that point our life will be a bright beacon that can guide our fellowmen toward inner peace and true happiness.

One of the most valuable things we can share with others is our testimony—our belief in God and Jesus Christ and in Their love for us. Elder John A. Widtsoe spoke of an agreement we made with Heavenly Father before coming to earth that we would help all of His sons and daughters:

> In our preexistent state, in the day of the great council, we made a[n] . . . agreement with the Almighty. The Lord proposed a plan . . . [and] we accepted it. . . . We agreed, right then and there, to be not only saviors for ourselves but . . . saviors for the whole human family. We went into a partnership with the Lord. The working out of the plan became then not merely the Father's work, and the Savior's work, but also our work. The least of us, the humblest, is in partnership with the Almighty in achieving the purpose of the eternal plan of salvation. That places us in a very responsible attitude towards the human race. By that doctrine, with the Lord at the head, we become saviors on Mount Zion, all committed to the great plan of offering salvation to the untold numbers of spirits. To do this is the Lord's self-imposed duty, this great labor his highest glory. Likewise, it is man's duty, self-imposed, his pleasure and joy, his labor, and ultimately his glory.[132]

Additionally, the responsibility to share the good news of the gospel belongs to each of us. Elder Alexander B. Morrison taught, "The very purpose of The Church of Jesus Christ of Latter-day Saints [is] to invite, encourage, and assist all of God's children, both living and dead, to come to Christ" (*Ensign,* Nov. 1987, 25).

FAMILY SURVEY REVIEW
Statement 24: We share the gospel with others.

- What are some of the ways our family shares the gospel with others?
- How can sharing the gospel strengthen our own faith?

STORY

Relate this fictionalized story to open a family discussion:

> My name is Melissa Jenkins and I am eleven years old. I live in Glenwood, California. I am one of only six Latter-day Saints in my school. This has been a big change for me because I recently moved here from Utah. Since not many people in my school know about the Church, I have lots of chances to do missionary work.
>
> I wear my CTR ring to school every day. Kids look at my ring and ask what CTR stands for. I always say, "Choose the right." And they say, "Cool!"
>
> One day, my friend Kimberly noticed my CTR ring and asked what it meant. I answered, "Choose the right." Kimberly said, "Awesome! How can I get one?"
>
> I told her that I got the ring from church. Kimberly asked me how much it cost and if she could buy one. I told her I'd get her one for free, and she was so excited.

I got a CTR ring from my Primary teacher on Sunday and took it to school on Monday. Kimberly thanked me about a hundred times! She kept wearing it every day and told me how awesome it was and how much she loved it.

A few days later another friend, named Michelle, also noticed my CTR ring. She saw that Kimberly had one too. Michelle thought our rings were cool and asked if she could get one.

Now, since she started wearing the ring, when Michelle takes the Lord's name in vain she quickly remembers and says, "Oh! I'm sorry!" When other kids swear around me Michelle says, "Don't swear around Melissa. She doesn't like it, and it's not choosing the right!"

It's nice to know that even though my friends don't belong to my church, they still want to choose the right and stand up for me. I've learned from living here and having friends who aren't LDS that most people are really good folks who are trying to do good things with their lives. I hope that the CTR rings keep helping Kimberly and Michelle and that I can be a good missionary no matter how old I get.

DISCUSSION

 1. How was Melissa a good missionary?
 2. How can we be good missionaries?

ACTIVITY

The activity for this lesson is to gather as a family and share how we feel about Heavenly Father. Then, let's discuss our feelings about the progress we've made toward our family goals. Third, let's talk about some of the important things we've learned from *Solutions for LDS Families*.

ASSIGNMENT

Read the Additional Solution for Success: Sharing Strengthens Families. Since this is the last assignment in *Solutions for LDS Families,* you may wish to share the program with another family. If you've benefited from the lessons and gained strength from the concepts, perhaps you can share your insights and experiences with others.

May the Lord's richest blessings be yours as you bless the lives of those around you.

ADDITIONAL SOLUTION FOR SUCCESS
SHARING STRENGTHENS FAMILIES

As family members we shouldn't simply focus on our desires alone. We need to think beyond ourselves and give to others. Creating a good family requires service and sacrifice, but joy always comes from loving and serving others. No matter what our circumstances, we can each give of ourselves and share something every day of our lives. We can share a smile, a warm greeting, a kind word, a listening ear. Albert Schweitzer once wrote, "Open your eyes and look for a human being, or some work devoted to human welfare, which needs from someone a little time or friendliness, a little sympathy, or sociability, or labour. . . . Search, then, for some investment for your humanity."[133]

The following story about a sister and brother helps us understand that the most important way we can give is to share a part of ourselves.

The violent grinding of brakes suddenly applied and the harsh creaking of skidding wheels gradually died away as the big car came to a stop. Eddie quickly picked himself up from the dusty pavement where he had been thrown and looked wildly around.

Linda! Where was the little sister he had been holding by the hand when they started to cross the street? The next moment he saw her under the big car that had run them down. With one bound, the boy was under the car, trying to lift the child.

"You'd better not try, son," said a man gently. "Someone has gone for help."

"She's not . . . dead, is she?" Eddie begged.

The man stooped and felt the limp little pulse. "No, my boy," he said slowly.

A policeman came, dispersed the collecting crowd, and carried the unconscious girl into a nearby store. Eddie's folded coat made a pillow for her head until the ambulance arrived. He was permitted to ride in the ambulance with her to the hospital. Something about the sturdy, shabbily dressed boy, only ten years old, and his devotion to his little sister touched the hearts of the hospital attendants.

"We must operate at once," said the surgeon after a brief preliminary examination. "She has been injured internally and has lost a great deal of blood." He turned to Eddie who stood close by. "How can we contact your parents?"

Eddie told him that their father was dead and that their mother did day work. He didn't know where.

"We can't wait to find her," said the surgeon, "because by that time it might be too late."

Eddie waited in the sitting area while the surgeons worked on Linda. After what seemed like an eternity, a nurse emerged from the operating room.

"Eddie," she said kindly, "your sister is doing very badly, and the doctor wants to give her a transfusion. Do you know what that is?" Eddie shook his head. "Linda has lost so much blood she cannot live unless someone gives her his. Will you do it for her?"

Eddie's face grew paler, and he gripped the knobs of the chair hard. For a moment he hesitated; then gulping back his tears, he nodded and stood up.

"That's a good boy," said the nurse.

She patted his head and led the way to the elevator, which took them to the operating room. No one spoke to Eddie except the nurse, who directed him in a low voice how to prepare for the ordeal. The boy bit his quivering lip and obeyed.

"Are you ready?" asked a man dressed in white, turning from the table over which he had been working. For the first time Eddie noticed Linda lying perfectly still on the table. His little sister—and he was going to make her well!

Eddie stepped forward quickly.

Two hours later the surgeon looked up with a smile into the faces of the young interns and nurses who were engrossed in watching the great man work.

"Fine," he said. "I think she will live."

After the transfusion Eddie had been told to lie quietly on a cot in the corner of the room. In the concern for the delicate operation Eddie had been forgotten.

"It was wonderful, Doctor!" exclaimed one of the young interns. "A miracle!"

"I am well satisfied," said the surgeon with pride.

There was a tug at his sleeve, but he didn't notice. In a little while there was another tug, and the great surgeon glanced down to see a pale-faced boy looking steadily up into his face.

"Doctor," said Eddie timidly, "when do I die?"

The interns laughed and the surgeon smiled. "Why, what do you mean, my boy?" he asked kindly.

"I thought—when they took somebody's blood—he died," muttered Eddie.

The smiles faded from the lips of the doctors and nurses, and the young intern caught his breath suddenly. This young boy had climbed to the very height of nobility and sacrifice and had showed them a glimpse of the greatest miracle of all—unconditional love.

There was a long pause before the surgeon answered softly, "You will both get well, Eddie—you and your little sister."

All who witnessed Eddie's act of selfless giving would never forget him.[134]

SOLUTIONS THROUGH STORIES AND POEMS: SPIRITUALITY

LOVE YOUR FELLOWMAN

Six generations of my father's ancestors lived in the little village of Scheveningen [Holland] at the seashore. They were fishermen or had other related vocations, like fishing-boat builders, sailmakers, or fishing-net repairmen. Many of them were also involved in the voluntary but hazardous task of lifesaving. They were stouthearted, experienced men who were always ready to man and row lifeboats for rescue missions. With every westerly gale that blew, some fishing boats ran into difficulties, and many times the sailors had to cling to the rigging of their stricken ships in a desperate fight to escape inevitable drowning. Year after year the sea claimed its victims.

On one occasion during a severe storm, a ship was in distress, and a rowboat went out to rescue the crew of the fishing boat. The waves were enormous, and each of the men at the oars had to give all his strength and energy to reach the unfortunate sailors in the grim darkness of the night and the heavy rainstorm.

The trip to the wrecked ship was successful, but the rowboat was too small to take the whole crew in one rescue operation. One man had to stay behind on board because there simply was no room for him; the risk that the rescue boat would capsize was too great. When the rescuers made it back to the beach, hundreds of people were waiting for them with torches to guide them in the dreary night. But the same crew could not make the second trip because they were exhausted from their fight with the stormwinds, the waves, and the sweeping rains.

So the local captain of the coast guard asked for volunteers to make a second trip. Among those who stepped forward without hesitation was a nineteen-year-old youth by the name of Hans. With his mother he had come to the beach in his oilskin clothes to watch the rescue operation.

When Hans stepped forward his mother panicked and said, "Hans, please don't go. Your father died at sea when you were four years old and your older brother Pete has been reported missing at sea for more than three months now. You are the only son left to me!"

But Hans said, "Mom, I feel I have to do it. It is my duty." And the mother wept and restlessly started pacing the beach when Hans boarded the rowboat, took the oars, and disappeared into the night.

After a struggle with the high-going seas that lasted for more than an hour (and to Hans's mother it seemed an eternity), the rowboat came into sight again. When the rescuers had approached the beach close enough so that the captain of the coast guard could reach them by shouting, he cupped his hands around his mouth and called vigorously against the storm, "Did you save him?"

And then the people lighting the sea with their torches saw Hans rise from his rowing bench, and he shouted with all his might, "Yes! And tell Mother it is my brother Pete!"

—Elder Jacob de Jager (*Ensign*, Nov. 1976, 56–57)

THE FIRST MISSIONARY JOURNEY OF SAMUEL SMITH

Samuel Smith, the first missionary of the Church, had the following interesting experience, told by his mother, Lucy Mack Smith:

On the thirtieth of June [1830], Samuel started on the mission to which he had been set apart by Joseph, and in traveling twenty-five miles, which was his first day's journey, he stopped at a number of places in order to sell his books [Book of Mormon], but was turned out-of-doors as soon as he declared his principles. When evening came on, he was faint and almost discouraged, but coming to an inn which was surrounded with every appearance of plenty, he called to see if the landlord would buy one of his books. . . a history of the origin of the Indians.

"I do not know," replied the host; "how did you get hold of it?"

"It was translated," rejoined Samuel, "by my brother, from some gold plates that he found buried in the earth."

"You liar!" cried the landlord, "get out of my house—you shan't stay one minute with your books." So saying, he thrust the young elder from a door of plenty. . . .

Samuel was sick at heart, for this was the fifth time he had been turned out of doors that day. He left the house, and traveled a short distance, and washed his feet in a small brook as a testimony against the man. He then proceeded five miles further on his journey, and seeing an apple tree a short distance from the road, he concluded to pass the night under it; and here he lay all night upon the cold, damp ground.[135]

Elder Carter E. Grant told the rest of the story:

> Following an arduous missionary trip that appeared to be a complete failure, Samuel returned home, carrying all his books but two. One he had given to a poor widow who fed him; the other he had presented to a new friend, John P. Green, a Methodist minister and a brother-in-law to Brigham Young. Mr. Green, after listening to Samuel's earnest testimony, read the book prayerfully and received a conviction of its truthfulness.
>
> Eagerly, he carried the new volume to his brother-in-law, Phineas H. Young, who also read and believed. Phineas in turn presented it to his brother, Brigham, who likewise read and received a testimony of its divinity. The acceptance of that sacred volume of "American scripture" started Brigham Young along the road to a famous destiny—one that was to influence greatly the history of the new Church as well as the history of Western America. This same book also helped to convert Heber C. Kimball. And in less than two years, the Greens, the Kimballs, and the Youngs, together with their households, were baptized. Thus, did Samuel, a young, unselfish servant of God, cast bread upon the waters to find it returned a hundredfold.[136]

FOR THE SAKE OF GIVING

John Chapman, a nurseryman in Pennsylvania, loved all the beautiful things in the world. He especially loved his great apple orchards when they were in bloom in the spring and when they were loaded with luscious fruit in the fall. He wished everyone could have an apple orchard. He was generous with the young trees and apple seeds. To the many families moving west, to make new homes, who came to buy young trees, he gave apples [and seeds] for their journeys . . . as well as saplings for the orchards they would start in distant prairie lands.

When discouraging letters came back to him stating that the saplings and seeds did not grow, he felt that it was because the pioneers did not know how to care for their young orchards. This worried him. He thought of the blessings apple orchards would be out in the new country.

He decided he must go himself to the new frontier. It was "as if he heard a call to go and plant orchards in the new land, to give apple trees to the pioneers." So John Chapman dedicated the rest of his life to giving.

He collected all the apple seeds he could buy or beg and made arrangements so that he could send for more. Then he went out into the wilderness, vowing that with God's help he would give the flowers and the fruit of a thousand orchards to the discouraged homesteaders.

He endured many hardships and dangers as he traveled. He planted orchards next to isolated cabins and churches, and in many communities. As the orchards grew they helped to bring love and hope and joy where there had been only bitterness and despair.

As the years went by, the trees in orchard after orchard took root and bore blossoms and fruit. The settlers named him Johnny Appleseed. He had the satisfaction of knowing that he had given a priceless gift to humanity. He said that the only reward he hoped for was that there would be orchards to plant and nurture in heaven. Truly Johnny Appleseed gave of himself for the sake of giving.

—Contributed by Eleanor Atkinson[137]

THE TOUCH OF THE MASTER'S HAND

'Twas battered and scarred, and the auctioneer
Thought it scarcely worth his while
To waste much time on the old violin,
But held it up with a smile:
"What am I bidden, good folks," he cried,
"Who'll start the bidding for me?"
"A dollar, a dollar"; then, "Two!" "Only two?
Two dollars, and who'll make it three?
Three dollars, once; three dollars, twice;
Going for three—" But no,
From the room, far back, a gray-haired man
Came forward and picked up the bow;
Then, wiping the dust from the old violin,
And tightening the loose strings,
He played a melody pure and sweet
As a caroling angel sings.
The music ceased, and the auctioneer,
With a voice that was quiet and low,
Said, "What am I bid for the old violin?"
And he held it up with the bow.
"A thousand dollars, and who'll make it two?
Two thousand! And who'll make it three?
Three thousand, once, three thousand, twice,

And going, and gone!" said he.
The people cheered, but some of them cried,
"We do not quite understand
What changed its worth." Swift came the reply:
"The touch of a master's hand."
And many a man with life out of tune,
And battered and scarred with sin,
Is auctioned cheap to the thoughtless crowd,
Much like the old violin.
A "mess of pottage," a glass of wine,
A game—and he travels on.
He's "going" once, and "going" twice,
He's "going" and almost "gone."
But the Master comes, and the foolish crowd
Never can quite understand
The worth of a soul and the change that's wrought
By the touch of the Master's hand.

—Myra Brooks Welch[138]

A Prayer

Where there is hatred, let me sow love. Where there is injury, pardon. Where there is doubt, faith. Where there is despair, hope. Where there is darkness, light. Where there is sadness, joy. O divine Master, grant that I may not so much seek to be consoled as to console; to be understood, as to understand; to be loved, as to love; for it is in giving that we receive; it is in pardoning that we are pardoned, and it is in dying that we are born to Eternal Life.

—St. Francis of Assisi1[139]

A Prayer for Parents

O! Give me patience when little hands,
Tug at me with ceaseless small demands.
O! Give me gentle words and smiling eyes,
And keep my lips from hasty sharp replies.
Let me not in weariness, confusion or noise,
Obscure my vision from life's few fleeting joys.
Then when in years to come, my home is still,
No bitter memories, its rooms may fill.

—Author Unknown[140]

I KNELT TO PRAY

I knelt to pray as day began
And prayed, "O God, bless every man.
Lift from each weary heart some pain
And let the sick be well again."

And then I rose to meet the day
And thoughtlessly went on my way:
I didn't try to dry a tear
Or take the time a grief to hear.
I took no steps to ease the load
Of hard-pressed travelers on the road;
I didn't even go to see
The sick friend who lives next door to me.

But then again when the day was done
I prayed, "O God, bless everyone."
But as I prayed a voice rang clear
Instructing me to think and hear.

"Consult your own heart ere you pray;
What good have you performed today?
God's choicest blessings are bestowed
On those who help him bear the load."

And then I hid my face and cried,
"Forgive me, Lord, for I have lied.
Let me live another day
And I will live it as I pray."

—Contributed by Sterling W. Sill[141]

HIGH RESOLVE

I'll hold my candle high, and
Then perhaps I'll see the hearts of men
Above the sordidness of life,
Beyond misunderstandings, strife.
Though many deeds that others do
Seem foolish, rash and sinful, too,
Just who am I to criticize
What I perceive with my dull eyes?
I'll hold my candle high, and then
Perhaps I'll see the hearts of men.

—Author Unknown[142]

EVALUATION

Congratulations! You have made a remarkable effort as you've worked through *Solutions for LDS Families*. Be confident in the knowledge that as you strengthen your family, our world becomes a better place. President James E. Faust remarked, "The family is far and away the greatest social unit, the best answer to human problems, in the history of mankind" (*Ensign*, May 1987, 82).

If you have completed the book, your family has read lessons on kindness, commitment, communication, choices, well-being, and spirituality. You have participated in many activities and discussions relating to these subjects.

Please return now to the Family Survey at the beginning of the book. To complete the *Solutions for LDS Families* activities, all family members should retake the survey. Answer all of the questions again. Make a new graph and talk about the progress you've made toward your goals.

As a family, discuss what you have learned as you've participated in the activities and lessons from *Solutions for LDS Families*. Continue using the resources in the book: the lessons, Additional Solutions for Success, and the many stories, poems, and activities.

If you have any stories, information, or "solutions for success" that can strengthen other families, I invite and encourage you to share them. To send your material or receive more information about the Solutions for Families programs, contact:

FAMILIES NOW Inc.
P.O. Box 37
Austin, Texas 78767-0037

In conclusion, I would like to thank all who contributed to *Solutions for LDS Families*, especially my sweet family. Additionally, I would like to thank you, the reader and participant. Without your interest and desire to strengthen your family, my efforts to share would be futile.

I offer a heartfelt prayer that our Heavenly Father's richest blessings will be with my brothers and sisters worldwide who obediently and courageously strive to magnify their stewardships as fathers, mothers, sons, and daughters—who work each day to strengthen their families and reach out to strengthen others. I applaud you and admire you! Don't hesitate to contact me with your family successes and challenges.

ENDNOTES

1. Thomas R. Lee et al., "The Family Profile II: A Self-Scored Brief Family Assessment Tool," Psychological Reports Journal 81, no. 2 (1997): 467–77.

2. Ibid., 1.

3. Ibid.

4. Letter in James R. Clark, ed., *Messages of the First Presidency of The Church of Jesus Christ of Latter-day Saints* (Salt Lake City: Bookcraft, 1970), 4:339.

5. Edward L. Kimball, ed., *The Teachings of Spencer W. Kimball* (Salt Lake City: Bookcraft, 1982), 120.

6. Clyde J. Williams, comp., *The Teachings of Lorenzo Snow* (Salt Lake City: Bookcraft, 1984), 62.

7. Jack M. Lyon et al., eds., *Best-Loved Poems of the LDS People* (Salt Lake City: Deseret Book, 1996), 126–27.

8. Glenn Van Ekeren, ed., *Speaker's Sourcebook II: Quotes, Stories, and Anecdotes for Every Occasion* (Paramus, N.J.: Prentice-Hall, 1994), 217.

9. Russell Lynes, "The Art of Acceptance," *Vogue,* 1 Sept. 1952, 206.

10. Spencer W. Kimball, *The Miracle of Forgiveness* (Salt Lake City: Bookcraft, 1969), 105.

11. Jack Canfield et al., eds., *A 4ᵗʰ Course of Chicken Soup for the Soul* (Deerfield Beach, Fla.: Health Communications, Inc., 1997), 78–79.

12. Van Ekeren, ed., *Speaker's Sourcebook II,* 217.

13. Canfield et al., eds., *A 4ᵗʰ Course of Chicken Soup for the Soul,* 85–86.

14. Van Ekeren, ed., *Speaker's Sourcebook II,* 123.

15. Quoted by Robert D. Hales, *Ensign,* May 1999, 33.

16. N. R. Spinner and L. Siegel, "Nonorganic Failure to Thrive," *Journal of Preventive Psychiatry* 3, no. 3 (1987): 279–87.

17. Canfield et al., eds., *Chicken Soup for the Mother's Soul* (1997), 203.

18. Stan Miller et al., eds., *Especially for Mormons, Volume Four* (Provo, Utah: Kellirae Arts, 1978), 271.

19. Adapted from Helen Keller, *The Story of My Life* (Garden City, N.Y.: Doubleday, 1955), 40–41.

20. Miller et al., eds., *Especially for Mormons, Volume Two* (1973), 289.

21. Miller et al., eds., *Especially for Mormons, Volume Four,* 169.

22. Miller et al., eds., *Especially for Mormons, Volume Two,* 200.

23. Dale Carnegie, *How to Win Friends and Influence People* (New York: Pocket Books, 1981), 70.

24. Glen Campbell, from his song "Less of Me," on the album *The Early Years.*

25. Lyon et al., eds., *Best-Loved Poems of the LDS People,* 288–89.

26. Miller et al., eds., *Especially for Mormon, Volume Four,* 129.

27. Van Ekeren, ed., *Speaker's Sourcebook II,* 68.

28. *Brigham Young University 1976 Speeches of the Year* (Provo, Utah: University Publications, 1997), 148.

29. Bryce J. Winkel and Barbara A. Winkel, *Isn't It about Time for Your Marriage?* (Beaverton, Ore.: Winco Publishing, 1991), 21.

30. Ibid., 22.

31. Ibid.

32. *Marriage and Family Relations: Participant's Study Guide* (Salt Lake City: The Church of Jesus Christ of Latter-day Saints, 2000), 46.

33. Canfield et al., eds., *Chicken Soup for the Mother's Soul,* 218–19.

34. Van Ekeren, ed., *Speaker's Sourcebook II,* 174.

35. Quote found online at http://www.quotations.usagreetings.com/html/attitude.html as recently as 19 May 2003.

36. Van Ekeren, ed., *Speaker's Sourcebook II,* 175.

37. *A Speaker's Sourcebook for Latter-day Saints* (Salt Lake City: Aspen Books, 1991), 157.

38. Adapted from Van Ekeren, ed., *Speaker's Sourcebook II,* 177.

39. Adapted from Miller et al., eds., *Especially for Mormons, Volume 1* (1971), 334–35.

40. Adapted from Helen Ream Bateman, *Roots and Wings* (Salt Lake City: Deseret Book, 1983), 48–50.

41. Miller et al., eds., *Especially for Mormons, Volume Three* (1976), 70–71.

42. Ibid., 103.

43. From Erma Bombeck's original syndicated column, Nov. 1971.

44. Lyon et al., eds., *Best-Loved Poems of the LDS People,* 208–9.

45. Miller et al., eds., *Especially for Mormons, Volume Two,* 69–70.

46. Miller et al., eds., *Especially for Mormons, Volume One,* 36.

47. Lyon et al., eds., *Best-Loved Poems of the LDS People,* 217–18.

48. Adapted from *Celebrating Family Strengths: Facilitator Manual* (Norman, Okla.: Southwest Prevention Center, University of Oklahoma, n.d.), 142.

49. Van Ekeren, *Speaker's Sourcebook II,* 70.

50. Ibid., 74.

51. Canfield et al., eds., *A 3rd Serving of Chicken Soup for the Soul* (1996), 78.

52. Adapted from *Celebrating Family Strengths,* 145.

53. Adapted from Van Ekeren, ed., *Speaker's Sourcebook II,* 75.

54. Adapted from *Celebrating Family Strengths,* 135.

55. Canfield et al., eds., *A 3rd Serving of Chicken Soup for the Soul,* 223–24.

56. Miller et al., eds., *Especially for Mormons, Volume Two,* 296.

57. Emerson Roy West, ed., *Vital Quotations* (Salt Lake City: Bookcraft, 1968), 171.

58. Miller et al., eds., *Especially for Mormons, Volume Three,* 158.

59. Lyon et al., eds., *Best-Loved Poems of the LDS People,* 25.

60. Miller et al., eds., *Especially for Mormons, Volume Four,* 135.

61. Taught to the author by her mother.

62. Lyon et al., eds., *Best-Loved Poems of the LDS People,* 123.

63. Ibid., 7–8.

64. Marcus Aurelius Antonius, *Meditations,* book 4 section 7.

65. Attributed to Lincoln by his friend Francis Carpenter. See Gabor S. Boritt et al., eds., *Of the People, by the People, for the People and Other Quotations by Abraham Lincoln* (New York: Columbia University Press, 1996), xvii.

66. Carnegie, *How to Win Friends and Influence People,* 67.

67. See Viktor E. Frankl, *Man's Search for Meaning* (New York: Washington Square Press, 1984).

68. Linda Kavelin Popov, *The Family Virtues Guide* (New York: Penguin, 1997), 225.

69. Miller et al., eds., *Especially for Mormons, Volume Four,* 298.

70. Bruce R. McConkie, *Mormon Doctrine* (Salt Lake City: Bookcraft, 1966), 539.

71. Van Ekeren, ed., *Speaker's Sourcebook II,* 63.

72. Bernie Boswell, *Families in Focus: Seven Secrets to a Successful Family* (n.p.: The Cottage Program International, 1992), 81.

73. Abraham Lincoln's last public address, 11 April 1865, in Boritt et al., eds., *Of the People, by the People, for the People and Other Quotations by Abraham Lincoln,* 112.

74. Boswell, *Families in Focus,* 82.

75. Miller et al., eds., *Especially for Mormons, Volume Three,* 82.

76. Adapted from Van Ekeren, ed., *Speaker's Sourcebook II,* 305.

77. Nick Stinnett and John DeFrain, *Secrets of Strong Families* (Boston: Little, Brown, 1985), 118.

78. Discussion adapted from Boswell, *Families in Focus,* 125–27.

79. David O. McKay, *Gospel Ideals* (Salt Lake City: Improvement Era, 1953), 5.

80. Canfield et al., eds., *Condensed Chicken Soup for the Soul* (1996), 140–41.

81. Miller et al., eds., *Especially for Mormons, Volume Two,* 155.

82. Story available online at http://www.websites-host.com/insp/istories.html as recently as 19 May 2003.

83. Lyon et al., eds., *Best-Loved Poems of the LDS People,* 252.

84. Ibid., 114.

85. Ibid., 100.

86. Ibid., 307.

87. Clare Middlemiss, comp., *Man May Know for Himself: Teachings of President David O. McKay* (Salt Lake City: Deseret Book, 1967), v.

88. *Celebrating Family Strengths,* 195.

89. *Teachings of the Presidents of the Church: Joseph F. Smith* (Salt Lake City: The Church of Jesus Christ of Latter-day Saints, 1998), 328–29.

90. *Teachings of the Presidents of the Church: Brigham Young* (Salt Lake City: The Church of Jesus Christ of Latter-day Saints, 1997), 194.

91. *Teachings of Gordon B. Hinckley* (Salt Lake City: Deseret Book, 1997), 172.

92. Rick Walton and Fern Oviatt, eds., *Stories for Mormons* (Salt Lake City: Bookcraft, 1983), 9.

93. Quote found online at http://www.brainyquote.com/quotes/quotes/a/q131187.html as recently as 19 May 2003.

94. Quote found online at http://www.brainyquote.com/quotes/quotes/e/q104269.html as recently as 19 May 2003.

95. Miller et al., eds., *Especially for Mormons, Volume Four,* 110–11.

96. Adapted from Boswell, *Families in Focus,* 69.

97. Adapted from Willam J. Bennet, *The Book of Virtues* (New York: Touchstone, 1993), 354–55.

98. Bernard E. Poduska, *For Love and Money* (Pacific Grove, Calif.: Brooks/Cole Publishing Co., 1993), 109.

99. "A Little Parable for Mothers," *Good Housekeeping,* May 1933, 19.

100. Miller et al., eds., *Especially for Mormons, Volume Four,* 132–33.

101. James E. Faust, *Stories from My Life* (Salt Lake City: Deseret Book, 2001), 123–24.

102. Miller et al., eds., *Especially for Mormons, Volume Two,* 117–18.

103. Lyon et al., eds., *Best-Loved Poems of the LDS People,* 200.

104. Ibid., 20–21.

105. Bryan B. Gardner and Calvin T. Broadhead, comp., *A Collection of Inspirational Verse for Latter-day Saints* (Salt Lake City: Bookcraft, 1963), 69.

106. Adrian Rogers, *Ten Secrets for a Successful Family* (Wheaton, Ill.: Crossway Books, 1996), 96.

107. Van Ekeren, ed., *Speaker's Sourcebook II,* 218.

108. Ibid.

109. Retold story. See alternate version in Canfield et al., eds., *5th Portion of Chicken Soup for the Soul* (1998), 108–16.

110. Quoted in the *New Era,* Nov. 1980, 47.

111. Kathleen Bahr, "Work in the Home: Building Enduring Relationships," unpublished lecture, given frequently at BYU. Excerpts taken from March 1999 World Congress of Families in Geneva, Switzerland.

112. C. S. Lewis, *The Screwtape Letters* (New York: Touchstone, 1996), 54.

113. Henry B.Eyring, *To Draw Closer to God* (Salt Lake City: Deseret Book, 1997), 98.

114. Victor B. Cline, *How to Make Your Child a Winner* (New York: Walker and Company, 1980), 242.

115. Letter in Clark, ed., *Messages of the First Presidency of The Church of Jesus Christ of Latter-day Saints,* 4:339.

116. Bruce R. McConkie, *A New Witness for the Articles of Faith* (Salt Lake City: Deseret Book, 1985), 21.

117. Miller et al., eds., *Especially for Mormons, Volume Two,* 114.

118. Gordon B. Hinckley, *Stand a Little Taller* (Salt Lake City: Eagle Gate, 2001), 194.

119. Miller et al., eds., *Especially for Mormons, Volume Three,* 256–57.

120. Larry Dossey, "Does Prayer Heal?" *Reader's Digest,* March 1996, 116–19.

121. Bruce R. McConkie address given 20 July 1971, in *BYU Speeches of the Year, 1970–71* (Provo, Utah: BYU Press, 1971), 6.

122. Adapted from Miller et al., eds., *Especially for Mormons, Volume Two,* 33.

123. Patrick Kavanaugh, *Spiritual Moments with the Great Composers* (Grand Rapids, Mich.: Zondervan, 1995), 158.

124. Ibid.

125. Ibid.

126. Ibid., 162.

127. Ibid., 166.

128. Ibid., 156.

129. Ibid., 31.

130. Ibid., 186–87.

131. Ibid., 31.

132. *Utah Genealogical and Historical Magazine,* Oct. 1934, 189.

133. Albert Schweitzer, *The Philosophy of Civilization,* trans. C. T. Campion (New York: Macmillan, 1960), 332.

134. Adapted from Canfield et al., eds., *Chicken Soup for the Soul* (1993), 27–28.

135. Carter Eldredge Grant, *The Kingdom of God Restored* (Salt Lake City: Deseret Book, 1955), 111–12.

136. Ibid., 112.

137. Adapted from Eleanor Atkinson, *Johnny Appleseed: The Romance of the Sower* (New York: Harper and Brothers, 1943).

138. Myra Brooks Welch, quoted by Boyd K. Packer, *Ensign,* May 2001, 22.

139. Miller et al., eds., *Especially for Mormons, Volume Two,* 246.

140. Ibid., 119.

141. Ibid., 226.

142. Miller et al., eds., *Especially for Mormons, Volume Four,*14.

About the Author

Paula Noble Fellingham has been extensively involved with many programs that strengthen families; most recently she has worked with Families Worldwide, Inc., eFamily.com, and Families Now, Inc. She also founded the nonprofit organization Solutions for Families, Inc., which currently endeavors to strengthen families in nations throughout the world.

Sister Fellingham was an educator for sixteen years and a daily radio show host. She is a veteran speaker at BYU Education Week and teaches with the "Know Your Religion" CES program of the Church. Additionally, Paula has taught part-time at Brigham Young University in the Marriage, Family, and Human Development Department. She is currently serving in the Church as a ward Relief Society president. Paula is the wife of Dr. Gilbert Fellingham and the mother of seven children.

If readers have any stories, information, or "solutions for success" that can strengthen other families, Paula invites and encourages families to share them. To send your material or receive more information, contact the author through Covenant Communications or visit www.solutionsforfamilies.com.